The Task of Christian Education

Theory and Design
of Christian Education Curriculum

BOOKS BY D. CAMPBELL WYCKOFF

Published by The Westminster Press

Theory and Design
    of Christian Education Curriculum

The Gospel and Christian Education

The Task of Christian Education

By D. CAMPBELL WYCKOFF

THEORY
and DESIGN
of
CHRISTIAN
EDUCATION
CURRICULUM

THE WESTMINSTER PRESS
Philadelphia

COPYRIGHT © MCMLXI W. L. JENKINS

All rights reserved—no part of this book may be reproduced in any form without permission in writing from the publisher, except by a reviewer who wishes to quote brief passages in connection with a review in magazine or newspaper.

LIBRARY OF CONGRESS CATALOG CARD NO. 61–6103

PRINTED IN THE UNITED STATES OF AMERICA

CONTENTS

CONCORDIA UNIVERSITY LIBRARY
PORTLAND OR 972..

CONTENTS

PREFACE

THE TIME HAS COME IN PROTESTANT CHRISTIAN EDUCATION FOR consolidation of the gains made in curriculum thinking and building and for the projection of next steps. The purpose of this book is to present a framework for curriculum thinking as complete, systematic, and useful as possible.

Although the author takes full responsibility for the book, he acknowledges that it is the product of a long process of co-operation among Protestant Christian educators who have had to do with curriculum in their denominations and in the National Council of the Churches of Christ in the United States of America. Permission has been granted to draw freely upon the materials and findings involved, with the understanding that sole responsibility for their use rests with the author.

The reader may be helped in understanding the positions that are taken in this book by reviewing the background of curriculum experience from which the book emerges. The author watched with great interest the first modern curriculum, *Christian Faith and Life: A Program for Church and Home*, come into being, studied the first proposals, and has worked more closely with it than with any other, as church school teacher, director, presbytery's committee chairman, and seminary professor.

He participated in the development of the special Indian American curriculum of the Board of National Missions of the Presbyterian Church in the U.S.A. during the 1940's and followed this up in two workshops at Ganado, Arizona, involving curriculum for Spanish-speaking people in the Southwest, Navaho Indian weekday curriculum, Christian education curriculum for Government Indian schools, and curriculum for mission high schools.

He has written curriculum materials, particularly the senior high unit *For Every Person* (Christian Board of Publication, 1959), based upon ideas in his *In One Spirit* (Friendship Press, 1958). Another major curriculum project in the area of senior high summer conference materials is planned for the near future.

His appetite for curriculum theory and design has been whetted by taking part in the National Council of Churches' studies of objectives, both senior high and general. This interest has developed to the present point as he has worked as consultant to the joint curriculum study of the Committee on the Graded Curriculum and the Committee on the Uniform Series. In connection with this consultative responsibility, a number of papers on curriculum theory and design have been prepared. These papers serve as a basis for the present book. While these studies have been going on, there has also been opportunity to participate in the National Council of Churches' youth study, a study that is pushing the findings of the work on objectives and curriculum on into the field of organization and program.

These studies, and the papers involved, have led to invitations from a number of denominational boards of education to engage in discussion of curriculum principles and problems with members of their staffs. Thus the opportunity has come to meet on this matter with staff members of the boards of the following communions: Methodist, Protestant Episcopal, United Church of Canada, Church of the Brethren, Presbyterian U.S., American Baptist, The American Lutheran Church,

and others in the United States and Canada on a more informal basis.

One of the most exciting and rewarding occasions on which
these matters have been discussed was a meeting for Methodist
missionaries and students from abroad, held at Lake Juna-
luska, North Carolina, in the summer of 1959. This provided
an excellent proving ground for the flexibility and universality
of the principles.

While this interest in curriculum was hinted at in *The Task
of Christian Education* (1955), it was much more fully developed in *The Gospel and Christian Education* (1959), in the
chapter "Educational Procedures in Light of the Gospel." The
opportunity to provide a brief synopsis of principles of curriculum theory and design was presented by the invitation to
write the chapter on curriculum for Marvin J. Taylor's *Religious Education: A Comprehensive Survey* (Abingdon Press,
1960). The present book represents a fuller exploration and
definition of these ideas.

If this book is to perform its proper function, it must be
approached, as were the papers that preceded it, as a "working
paper." The principles it enunciates, the ideas it presents, the
proposals it makes, must be reacted to, tried out, changed or
corrected if it is to serve as a means for the improvement of the
curriculum of Protestant education. One hopes that it may
stimulate other studies, particularly denominational and interdenominational studies, based in theology, Biblical research,
the behavioral sciences, and education.

When the current reconsideration of curriculum theory and
design was initiated by the National Council of Churches, the
question that needed to be answered was that of the kind of
curriculum needed in Protestantism now and in the future.
Over the months and years, intensive work has been done on
the foundations of curriculum in theology and in educational
theory, on objectives, on content, on the setting for curriculum,
on educational method, on curricular organization, and on
progression and adaptability. All these questions are dealt with

systematically in the present book in an attempt to reflect faith-
fully the work of the study and to interpret its findings so that
they may be available and useful to all who deal with curriculum, at whatever level.

If I were to mention all the persons who have contributed
their thought and criticism to this book, the list would be a
long and distinguished one, representative of all Protestant
Christian education in the United States and Canada. While
such a list cannot be included here, many will know that my
expression of sincere gratitude is meant for them, sometimes
for a telling word and sometimes for hours and days of painstaking study and criticism. The various denominations, the
National Council of Churches, and others have been consider-
ate in permitting me to use and quote from their statements
and documents. Special thanks go to the staff of the Department of Curriculum Development of the Division of Christian
Education of the National Council of Churches, whose members worked long and hard to help to bring this book into
being. The death of Mildred A. Magnuson, for ten years the
director of the Department of Curriculum Development, occurred just two days before the manuscript of this book was
completed; its publication is in no small part due to her faithful work on its behalf.

D. CAMPBELL WYCKOFF

PART
I

Background

Background...

"IS ECUMENICAL CURRICULUM POSSIBLE?" BY ASKING THIS question, although not directly of the Sunday church school, Iris V. Cully (in *Religion in Life,* Summer, 1960, pp. 426–433) points out two facts currently of extreme concern to Protestant curriculum.

First, there has been a "falling away of interdenominational co-operation in practical matters of religious education," due in part to "the growing emphasis on theological and Biblical interpretation within each denominational curriculum."

Second, there is a difference between the "interdenominational" and the "ecumenical" approaches, the former representing a "least common denominator" approach and the latter "making each person conscious of the unique witness of his own denomination to the total Christian community."

"Something," she concludes, "will have to happen soon. Many ministers and directors are eager for a different orientation in curriculum. . . . The possibility of such a change is hinted in the National Council's recent study outline, *The Objectives of Christian Education.*"

The purpose of this book is to try to answer the question of ecumenical curriculum with specific proposals based upon considered principles. If a convincing start can be made here,

Protestant churches may be encouraged to take the next steps, deciding on ways in which they may work together to make such curriculum available to the churches and going to work to prepare and produce it.

Parts II and III of this book deal systematically with theory and design. But before the specific principles and proposals may be discussed, there are three types of background materials that need to be brought into play: a definition of the place of the curriculum in the total task of the church's teaching ministry, salient events and developments in the history of Protestant curriculum, and the question of Christian education objectives.

Chapter 1 discusses the place of the curriculum in the task of Christian education. The nature and mission of the church require a teaching ministry. The teaching ministry calls for a planned approach to instruction and nurture in harmony with the church's purpose and task.

Chapter 2 deals with the history of Protestant curriculum, stressing in particular the events and trends that have led up to the present situation. Such a historical perspective may prevent the repetition of the past's costly mistakes and may indicate to contemporary Christian educators the nature of the strategic moment in which they work.

Chapter 3 raises the question of objectives. Whenever Protestant educators feel uneasy, they habitually turn to a restudy of objectives. Yet "objectives" means a great many different things. An attempt is made in this chapter to unravel these meanings and to show their significance for the present curriculum undertaking.

Chapter 1

THE CURRICULUM AND THE TASK
OF CHRISTIAN EDUCATION

THE TASK of Christian education is the nurture of the Christian life. In order that such nurture may be effective in accomplishing its purpose, the church as a rule rejects reliance upon haphazard means and adopts a reasoned and planned teaching-learning process for its educational work. A curriculum is a plan by which the teaching-learning process may be systematically undertaken.

Such a conception of curriculum, and its place in Christian nurture, is in harmony with the definition that has been used for some years: "Curriculum is experience under guidance toward the fulfillment of the purposes of Christian education —not the entire social situation within which the person acts and with which he is interacting, but rather that part of it which is consciously planned." (*A Guide for Curriculum in Christian Education,* p. 25).

A curriculum is a carefully devised channel of communication used by the church in its teaching ministry in order that the Christian faith and the Christian life may be known, accepted, and lived. The curriculum task is that of designing a plan for the communicative transaction, involving the various partners to the transaction but centering upon a learner or a learning group.

The Church, Its Mission, and Its Ministry

The communication of the Christian faith, the gospel, is the church's imperative. The church is that company of persons which has been called by God and drawn into a fellowship, in order to worship, witness, and work in Christ's name and by the power of the Holy Spirit. The church's first task is worship, a service that relates the Christian community to its Creator, Judge, Loving Father, Savior, and Source of Strength and guidance. The Quakers speak of "waiting for true concerns to arise from our worship and silence together." The church's second task, that of witness, is a matter of making its experience of reconciliation and redemption clear and compelling to its contemporaries, in order that this experience may be theirs also. The church's third task, that of work, means the active furthering of its mission and ministry in a variety of ways that are appropriate to its situation.

The mission of the church, according to *The Objectives of Christian Education* (p. 18), is to witness to the good news of God's redeeming love as revealed in the life, death, and resurrection of Jesus Christ; to hold out a continuing summons to the worship and service of God; to maintain and extend a fellowship in which persons, led by the Holy Spirit, may respond in faith to his transforming power; to help persons, both as individuals and in society, to develop such attitudes and relationships with God and one another as will lead to an increasing Christian witness through Christian life and service to human need; and to pray in word and deed, "Thy kingdom come."

This mission is to persons in a world where non-Christian faiths are experiencing a resurgence, where nationalism and race are major forces for rapid change, where political systems stand as bitter rivals and divide the world between them, where it has been said that the "one vital question" is war or peace in the face of the threat of the end of human existence by nuclear weapons, where people have lost their sense of the family and neighborhood, yet find it difficult to transcend the local in their interests and concerns, where philosophers fail to see reality beyond the moment, where science as a guide to life and truth is virtually unchallenged, and where psycho-analysts have assumed a priestly role. Persons in such a world need to discover themselves again, to grasp the nature of the situation in which they live, to regain a sense of community, to find and avail themselves of guidance that is both immediate and ultimate, to take on fitting and effective social responsi-bility, and to live now in terms of a final assurance.

The world is rediscovering the church, and the church is rediscovering itself, as the mission and ministry to the world and its need become evident and are pursued. The imperative to communicate the gospel is at the heart of mission and ministry, for the gospel shows us who we truly are, gives us the clue to our human situation, gathers us into a community of faith, witnesses to the presence and power of the Holy Spirit for the guidance of our personal and corporate experience, calls us to discipleship in meeting the world's needs together, and establishes our eternal hope. The gospel thus communi-cated is the renewing power that the church requires today. According to Reinhold Niebuhr, the imperative is "to relate the gospel to the culture of the age without losing its essential truth. . . . To validate the gospel in our civilization. . . . To apply the wisdom and power of the gospel to individual and collective human predicaments" (*The Christian Century,* June 18, 1958).

In the New Testament, the church's ministry is regarded as a gift or as a variety of gifts co-ordinated with one another. The diversity and unity of these gifts is likened to the diversity and unity of the parts and whole of the human body. The gift of apostleship, the gift of the prophet, the gift of the evangelist, the gift of the pastor, and the gift of the teacher add up to the essential work of the church. (Eph. 4: 1–16.) Since these are gifts, the persons who exercise the church's ministry in any way must receive as gifts the responsibility and power of ministry. No one can generate such power for himself.

But there is a prior gift, the ministry of the word. The word is God's creative power, the communication of his redeeming and reconciling purpose, the reality of Jesus Christ as the incarnate Lord, the witness to revelation and redemption in the Bible, and the witness of the Holy Spirit to the person who hears and believes. The ministry of the word is a gift to every Christian as he is aware of the gospel and is led to respond to it. The conditions of this ministry, the ways by which the gift is received and used, are faithfulness in study, faithfulness in communication, and faithfulness in community under the word. "The church exists to proclaim what God has done in the past, is doing today, and will do in the future."

In its current rediscovery and renewal, the church finds that its ministry is not so simple and clear-cut as it once supposed. The realization that all its members have a share in its ministry, while not a new idea, has the power to fire the contemporary church with a new sense of personal and collective vocation. James D. Smart has pointed out the difficulty of separating "the ministry of an ordained clergy and the ministry of the whole church," declaring that the Biblical idea of ministry is that: "All who responded in faith to Jesus Christ were called to minister and bear witness among their fellow men, but the Twelve, and others later, were chosen for a special ministry without which the church would not have long endured. . . . Baptism and confirmation are the primary ordination to the ministry of Jesus Christ to which all else is secondary. . . . One cannot be a Christian without receiving the Spirit of God, which is always empowerment for a ministry" (*The Rebirth of Ministry*, pp. 11–12).

THE EDUCATIONAL TASK

Christian education, as is pointed out in *The Objectives of Christian Education* (p. 19), is one of the ministries by which the church seeks to fulfill its nature and perform its mission. It is to be regarded not as merely a segment but as an integral part of the total work of the church, which includes many aspects, such as worship, the sacraments and ordinances, preaching, pastoral counseling, parish administration, evangelism, missions, stewardship, social action, and teaching. Each aspect ultimately involves all the others, each utilizes educational procedures, and each helps to achieve the aims of the church.

In addition to showing how the church's teaching ministry is related to its other ministries and to its total ministry, the same document defines Christian education (p. 18) as a means by which the church seeks to help persons respond to the gospel (the message of God's redeeming love revealed in Jesus Christ) and to grow in their understanding of its promises and acceptance of its claims. Christian education is a lifelong process by which persons are led to commitment to Jesus Christ through helping them to understand and accept the Christian faith and its implications for time and eternity and to an increasing understanding and more effective expression of Christian faith in relation to God and in all human relationships. To be effective, the document continues, Christian education must be grounded solidly in the Christian revelation, and it must minister to persons in the light of their individual maturity, physical and social environment, previous experience and training, ability to learn, and basic needs.

In the mid-1940's the Study of Christian Education produced a classic definition of Christian education which, although it does not identify Christian education by the term "ministry," does justice to its nature, responsibilities, and relationships:

Christian education is the process by which persons are confronted with and controlled by the Christian gospel. It involves the efforts of the Christian community to guide both young and adult persons toward an ever richer possession of the Christian heritage and a fuller participation in the life and work of the Christian fellowship. It is both individual and social in nature. It is individual, because it deals with persons, and each person is unique and different from all other persons. It is social, because it seeks to relate persons to the Christian community and to transform community life toward an ever fuller embodiment of Christian ideals. It is concerned with the past, the present, and the future—with the past, because it seeks to introduce persons to their religious heritage, with the present, because it aims to make religion a vital force in every response to life, with the future, because it cultivates creative experiences leading to growth in wisdom and stature and favor with God and man. (Paul H. Vieth, *The Church and Christian Education*, p. 52.)

In spite of the unfashionable terminology (such as "Christian ideals") and the lack of theological dimensions currently being stressed (such as the eschatological), this definition is sufficiently clear, comprehensive, and logical to be used by us as a basis for the Protestant curriculum enterprise today.

All education clearly implies a process of nurture toward an end. The end, the goal, gives it direction. Purposes determine to a large degree what shall be included in the educational process and in what order, what shall be stressed, and what shall be played down or omitted. This is fundamental, since education is a highly selective process, the time and resources at its disposal being limited and far-reaching results being demanded of it.

For Christian education the question, What is a Christian? is crucial, for upon it depends the purpose that will shape and guide its curriculum and all its other operations. The definition of "Christian" in the concordance of *The Westminster Study Edition of The Holy Bible* is: A Christian is "one who by faith in Christ as his Savior and Lord enters into fellowship with God, becomes a member of the body of Christ, and in the power of the Holy Spirit bears witness to Christ by word and life." This definition "checks out" in terms of the relevant Biblical material and in terms of Christian personality theory.

Furthermore, it is a definition with which one can work. Clearly the possibility of "being a Christian" is incomprehensible except in terms of the gracious work of God reflected in the act of faith, membership in the body of Christ, and bearing witness by the power of the Holy Spirit.

If this is what it means to be a Christian, there are pertinent questions to be raised immediately: How may I become a Christian? How may I be sustained as a Christian? These questions are of the most profound concern to the church's teaching ministry.

One of the definitive aspects of being a Christian, membership in the body of Christ, indicates that the Christian needs the church and the education it gives him, for it is the church that educates him as a Christian. Thus the teaching function (as is being convincingly pointed out in the current literature on the subject) is an indispensable responsibility of the church. But it is not the church's only function, and it is performed effectively only when there is complete co-ordination with the other functions by which the church nurtures the Christian life. (Rom. 12: 4-8; Eph. 4: 4-7, 11-13.)

As one engages in the exercise of the gifts of prophecy, service, teaching, exhorting, contributing, giving aid, and doing acts of mercy and in the apostolic, prophetic, evangelistic, pastoral, and teaching functions, he is "in Christ," a member of his body. The members are a co-ordinated unity at work, continuing Christ's ministry in the world. Along, then, with other indispensable functions, teaching (education, the teaching-learning process) is one of the functions of the community of men in Christ.

The teacher, as a working member of the body of Christ, engages in a shared ministry. The ministry is shared with others engaged in other ministries to be co-ordinated with his in the total mission and ministry of the church. The ministry is shared with other teachers working in the church and on behalf of the church. The ministry is shared with learners in a fellowship of work and worship involving leaders and followers, guides and students. "Speaking the truth in love, we are to grow up in every way into him who is the head, into Christ, from whom the whole body, joined and knit together by every joint with which it is supplied, when each part is working properly, makes bodily growth and upbuilds itself in love." (Eph. 4: 15–16.)

Using a slightly different analysis, James D. Smart opens his book *The Teaching Ministry of the Church* with an unequivocal statement of the principle involved: "The church of Jesus Christ has, of necessity, a teaching function. The church must teach, just as it must preach, or it will not be the church. . . . Teaching belongs to the essence of the church and a church that neglects this function of teaching has lost something that is indispensable to its nature as a church. It is a defective church if it is lacking at this point, just as a church in which the gospel ceases to be preached in its purity or a church in which the sacraments cease to be rightly administered is a defective church" (p. 11).

The point is made that the nurture of the Christian life, including nurture through education, is a necessary function of the redemptive community in Christ, the church; and that involved in becoming and being sustained as a Christian is responsible membership in that body, the responsible use of one's gifts in the upbuilding of the community of Christ's ministry, and full and lovingly responsive use of the gifts of the other members of the body. In these terms, the aims of the church's education, shared with the church's other functions, are:

> The equipment of the saints, . . . the work of ministry, . . . building up the body of Christ,

until we all attain

> to the unity of the faith and of the knowledge of the Son of God,

> to mature manhood,

to the measure of the stature of the fullness of Christ. (Eph. 4: 12–13.)

Once the hope, practice, and achievement of membership in Christ's body becomes a leading motif in education at every age and experience level (as it must become), the door is open and Christian education may step into its rightful place in the educational scene.

The climax, the very heart, of education is Christian education. Christian education seeks not just the useful life or the life of wisdom and dedication, but the reclaimed life, the life transformed by the God who created man in his own image, who revealed himself with redemptive clarity in Jesus Christ, and whose Holy Spirit guides those who see and respond. Christian education is not something that can be accomplished in one perfunctory hour each week, nor something to be attempted by half-trained or half-dedicated people. Persons are required who possess and know the reclaimed and redeemed life, and who are prepared to witness tellingly to their experience. Christian education is the work of those who, as the church, try to introduce persons to, and train them within, the transformed and reconstructed life that is found with God in Christ.

THE CURRICULUM

What, then, are the practical requirements for effective Christian education? By direct implication from what has already been said, eight prerequisites may be identified. None can stand alone. Although curriculum is only part of Christian education, each of these prerequisites has something essential to say to the curriculum theorist and designer.

Christian education requires a clear idea of the reason for Christian teaching and learning. The church, the minister, the educator, and the learner need to know what the teaching-learning process is supposed to accomplish in the Christian community. They need to know what it is and why it is essential.

Christian education requires a church that is truly the church of Jesus Christ at work. No educational process separated from a genuine community that embodies its purpose and meaning is likely to be effective.

Christian education requires a Christian home. In a sense the Christian home is the Christian church in one of its manifestations. The kind of home that plays its part in nurturing the Christian life is one in which the members play, work, think, talk, and pray together.

Christian education requires a church school that is a real school. In such a school serious study will take place, including study of the Bible, doctrine, history, and current affairs. Social action will be planned, carried out, and evaluated as an expression of the Christian mission. Fellowship will be one of the school's characteristics, enjoyment and fulfillment in the corporate Christian life. At the center will be worship, the direct service of God, search for his will, and dedication to it together.

Christian education requires sound instructional materials. Such materials will lead the pupils to live in Christ. In order that this may be realized, the materials will be theologically accurate, acquaint the pupil thoroughly with the Bible, teach churchmanship, observe the abilities and needs of the pupil in terms of grading, breathe an evangelistic spirit, and stress mission, stewardship, and social education and action.

Christian education requires a concern in and for the community. Concern in the community will be expressed by agencies and organizations more or less closely allied with the church in purpose and by a prevailing concern for Christian experience and values. Concern for the community will be expressed in terms of the church's fellowship and mission with those in its immediate environment.

Christian education requires the kind of building and the sorts of equipment that invite children, youth, and adults to venture into the Christian life; that help rather than hinder Christian teaching; and that stand both as tools and as symbols of the centrality of Christian nurture in the church that is the community of Christ.

Christian education requires intelligent, skilled, and dedicated administration. This requirement at present is the responsibility of the minister, the committee on Christian education, the superintendent, and the other officers.

If the curriculum of Christian education is a plan by which the teaching-learning process may be systematically undertaken in the Christian community, then all eight of these requirements are important to it. To isolate the curriculum problem as one of instructional materials alone reflects a mistaken notion of its meaning in the church's educational process.

Perhaps it would be well at this point to define certain key terms explicitly:

Curriculum: The plan and program by which the church seeks to fulfill its educational imperative. "Curriculum is experience under guidance toward the fulfillment of the purposes of Christian education—not the entire social situation within which the person acts and with which he is interacting, but rather that part of it which is consciously planned." The plan consists of educational procedures selected and used to help the learner to perceive, accept, and fulfill God's redeeming purpose in Jesus Christ.

Program: The activities and undertakings that constitute the church's total educational ministry for children, youth, adults, the family, and the congregation as a whole. In most cases "program" is synonymous with "curriculum" as defined above. The old administratively begotten distinction between curriculum as materials and program as activities is specifically rejected.

Curriculum theory: Curriculum theory consists of the principles that act as sound guides to curriculum practice: principles with respect to the orientation, design, and use and evaluation of the curriculum.

Curriculum design: Curriculum design involves the establishment of the blueprint for the educational program in terms of good principles of teaching and learning, the provision of guides for the various aspects of the program, and the provision of educational aids.

Curriculum content: The content of the curriculum consists of the scope of Christian education, the whole field of relationships in the light of the gospel, the great concerns of the Christian faith and the Christian life.

Curriculum materials: Curriculum materials are the resources (printed and otherwise) that are employed within "experience under guidance."

One of the most inclusive and accurate summaries of the place of the curriculum in the Christian education task is that developed in *The Objective of Christian Education for Senior High Young People* (p. 14), where it is stated: (1) Christian education, at whatever age level, is guided by one objective. (2) It takes place in a setting that consists of the whole field of relationships. (3) Its curriculum involves the undertaking of certain common and lifelong tasks. (4) Responsibility for it is shared by groups that cut across age-level boundaries.

Interpreted in this way, the curriculum has its absolute and unchangeable core (its essential message) and its situational side (its response and communication to the time and place in which it serves). As more and different needs that have to be met are discovered, the experiences through which the unchangeable core of the curriculum is communicated to the child, youth, and adult must be adapted. Methods also may be changed. Not all new methods will stand the test, but they have to be tried out, a variety of methods has to be used, and methods uniquely adapted to the interest and needs of the pupil have to be sought out in order that the process may be carried on at all successfully.

The contrasts of our time are forcing curriculum change,

and the curriculum needs to remain fluid in order that it may meet the challenge they present. Human knowledge is outrunning our ability to comprehend it, yet there is a renewed interest in theology and philosophy as disciplines that enable us to evaluate knowledge selectively if not to comprehend it completely in quantitative terms. Mass communications and means of travel have vastly increased our ability to transmit and receive stimuli and to go places speedily, yet this is counterbalanced by attention to selectivity and discrimination with regard to values. Ours is a divided world, yet there is a growing consciousness of the need for unity based upon trust and trustworthiness. The world in which we live is disrupted and its people are so mobile as to be rootless, yet there is an attempt to develop stability in our national and community life. Fear dominates the times, yet courage is emphasized, and access to the resources that make for courage is opened to children, youth, and adults. Lethargy is a prevalent blight, yet the times are challenging, and there are many seeking to meet the challenges presented. There is the loneliness of the mass and the multitude, yet every attempt is made to stress a real fellowship and unity among us.

The curriculum is a tool by which Christian education proposes, through the church, to deal with these contrasts of our time adequately by nurture that replaces incomprehensibility with understanding, diffuse overstimulation with calm concentration upon that which is worthy, social division with a new unity based on respect and truth, disruption with stability, fear with courage, lethargy with challenge, and loneliness with community. The curriculum, as it performs its function in Christian education, cannot be conceived narrowly any more but must be thought of as broadly as to include its role as the church's agent in helping the person to reorient his total education, and as broadly as to include the school of the church, the home, and even the college and university.

The curriculum of Christian education will be adequate to the times to the extent that through it the redemptive impact of the gospel is felt by the individual, the church, and society. Every educational activity must in reality be an expression of the community of Christians, the community of the faithful together with their children, studying together to learn of truth; deepening their fellowship; testing themselves and learning through remedial and constructive social action; and serving and gathering new direction and inspiration through common worship.

Chapter 2

HIGHLIGHTS IN THE HISTORY
OF PROTESTANT CURRICULUM

IN ORDER to assess the current need for curriculum change, it will be helpful to review pertinent historical developments. How has the changing scene (world, national, educational, and church) affected curriculum? What trends are discernible? What basic questions have been answered? What questions are still unanswered? What policies and plans are now being followed? Why? What changes are in the offing? What effects are they likely to have? What resources are available to us?

SOURCES OF THE PRESENT SITUATION

The patterns of ancient Jewish education may be inferred from the Old Testament. Deuteronomy 6: 1–9, for instance, presents a picture of the responsibility of the home for the most integral indoctrination in the law and ways of the people. In Ps. 78: 1–8, we are shown a way of dealing with the history of God and his people. During the exile the synagogue became the center of the community's education, its service being primarily didactic.

The early Christian church stressed adult education in the training of the catechumenate. In the service of the Mass there is a remnant of the ancient practice of preceding the Mass of

the faithful, which was sacramental, with the Mass of the cate-
chumens, which was instructional.

During the Middle Ages formal education was concentrated
in schools for the clergy, associated with the monasteries and
cathedrals. For ordinary persons, educational experience was
informal, consisting of person-to-person, word-of-mouth instruction. Undoubtedly the mystery plays, the art of the period,
and the historical and doctrinal material built into the great
churches had their educational influence. During this time the
universities came slowly into being, stressing theology, canon
law, the liberal arts, and later, science.

The Reformation saw a revival of preaching as a means of
instruction. The family was singled out as the most important
center of Christian training, especially by Luther. Most
churches devised rather elaborate systems of catechetical instruction and Biblical teaching. Specific moral instruction was
particularly associated with the Puritan tradition. During this
time the responsibility of the state for education was established in principle.

The early days in the United States witnessed the use of
the Bible and the catechisms in the common school. The Sunday school was adopted from Britain, its function being considerably altered when the public schools became stronger and
ceased to teach sectarian religion. Great lay interest in Christian education was manifested in the work of the American
Sunday School Union and later in the powerful National Sunday School Convention.

In 1869, seeking for a remedy for many prevailing ills
(particularly those of the "memory-work period"), the National
Sunday School Convention appointed a committee to prepare
a uniform lesson system. The system was to be uniform in the
sense that it would be suitable for use in any church and by all
age groups in the church. The organizing principle for the system was to be Biblical content. Other possible organizing principles that were rejected because they did not lend themselves
to uniformity included doctrine, Christian duties, and the

church year. In 1872, committees were appointed to prepare lessons to cover the Bible in a seven-year cycle (later changed to a six-year cycle), alternating between the Old and the New Testaments.

In 1908, in response to the demand for attention to the needs and capacities of the learner, the closely graded lessons were introduced, a permanent outline being used for each grade.

Group-graded lessons, based upon a three-year departmental cycle, were adopted officially in 1922, and were replaced by the "cycle-graded series" in 1945. They were based upon such educational principles as these: (1) the use of the Bible in relation to life situations at the various age levels; (2) the achievement of sequence, balance, and comprehensiveness by taking account of the maturing interests and experiences of the various age levels, the anticipation of emerging needs, and seasonal emphases; (3) the integration of the lessons with the total program of the age group.

In his book *A Social Theory of Religious Education* (1917), George Albert Coe devoted a chapter to "A New Theory of the Curriculum." The old theory was, in his words, "an imposition theory of the curriculum," because it was set and imposed upon the pupils by the teachers. A stereotyped rigidity characterized it, and whether it fitted with new surroundings and circumstances or not it was rigorously applied without any flexibility or preparation for accommodation. Over against this theory, Coe set a concept of curriculum concerned with living situations and interaction between personalities, directed toward developing interest and not merely feeding interests already present. For this purpose, the pupil's social activities in family, play group, and classroom were to be media for deepening co-operation. This was a "curriculum of social living."

George Herbert Betts, in *The Curriculum of Religious Education* (1924), developed a cultural theory of the curriculum. Culture is an evolved product of social life, and according to changing social conditions, cultural materials change in value. Hence the need for a selection of materials from the mass of cultural materials. "This selected and abridged body of subject matter when properly organized for the purposes of study, learning, and instruction, is called a curriculum." (P. 207.) In the determination of the curriculum, agencies, such as tradition, professional leadership, public demand, and the influence of public education all come into play. Betts saw three curricular objectives: (1) The curriculum must have definable, attainable, proved, and measurable goals. (2) The goals must be personal and child-centered. (3) It must meet the threefold need of the individual: knowledge; loyalty to causes, persons, and institutions; and religious values expressed in social and personal conduct.

An extremely influential position was expounded by William Clayton Bower in *The Curriculum of Religious Education* (1925). He pleaded for making experience the center of the curriculum. "The enrichment of experience is a concept that relates itself immediately to the self-realization of persons." (P. 93.) Experience is to be enriched and controlled under guidance. "An experience-curriculum will, then, consist of a body of carefully selected and organized experiences lifted out of the actual ongoing life of the person or social group; of a critical study of the situations themselves for their essential factors and their possible outcomes; of the ideas, ideals, attitudes, and habits that have emerged from the past experience of the learner and the vast stores of historical subject matter that have descended from generation to generation and that contain in organized and available forms the best that the race has thought and felt and purposed." (P. 179.)

An experience-curriculum, according to Bower, has to be dynamic since experiences and values are changing. But "a dynamic curriculum must be more than a follower of experience; it must anticipate experience and give it constructive direction."(P. 254.) The chief features of a dynamic curriculum are: (1) It creates conditions that lead to continuous growth. Learning should not be confined to the young. The highest process of learning is learning how to learn. (2) It creates a vital conception of truth. Truth calls forth not defense but understanding. A proper conception of truth will reveal that there is no conflict between scientific and religious truths. (3) It educates the tolerant mind and develops a respect for the other man's convictions. (4) It strives toward the responsible mind. (5) It is more forward-looking than backward-looking. It is more prophetic than priestly. The things and values of the past should have less importance than the unrealized values of the future, which culminate in the realization of the Kingdom of God. (6) It must aim at producing a creative attitude toward life.

In the midst of the ferment in curriculum represented by Coe, Betts, and Bower, the International Council of Religious Education came into being, as a merger of the major lay and denominational religious education organizations. One of the new council's first projects was to undertake the development of "The International Curriculum of Religious Education." This project was intended to provide a curriculum oriented to the experience of the learner as it grows out of his total interaction with his objective world. According to *The Development of a Curriculum of Religious Education* (1928):

> The objective of religious education from the viewpoint of the evangelical denominations is complete Christian living which includes personal acceptance of Jesus Christ as Savior and his way of life, and, under normal circumstances, membership in a Christian church; the Christian motive in the making of life choices; and wholehearted participation in and constructive contribution to the progressive realization of a social order controlled by Christian principles. (P. 38.)

To implement this objective specific objectives are to be discovered through a study of the experience of growing persons:

> In a general way, the direction of the educational process must be known from the beginning. No amount of study of

experience will serve to reveal what these ultimate outcomes should be. Objectives do not become specific, however, until they are considered in relation to the interests, activities, and needs of the learner. Thus a searching investigation into the life stream of the learner is essential to the process of establishing objectives. The general statements of desired outcomes serve as criteria for the evaluation of the situations of the learner, and the situations in turn serve to make the objectives specific and concrete. (P. 26.)

The form that this investigation into the life stream of the learner took was twofold: an analysis of areas of human experience and an analysis of Christian character traits. These were then developed into a crosshatch, so that the desirable and undesirable traits in various areas of experience would be defined. Curriculum implications for the development of these traits might then be drawn.

Although the theory of the International Curriculum made the mistake of identifying Christian education too closely with character education, a great deal of invaluable material on the developmental aspects of religious living was gathered in connection with the research involved with its preparation. In time, the idea of developing it into a curriculum was abandoned, and the material gathered was organized into a series of volumes known as *The International Curriculum Guide*. The gist of its findings was included in *The Curriculum Guide for the Local Church* (1945, revised 1950), and its successor, *A Guide for Curriculum in Christian Education* (1955).

The curriculum situation in the immediate past was shaped by the findings of the Study of Christian Education, summarized by Paul H. Vieth, in *The Church and Christian Education* (1947). In the Study, the theological movement made itself felt as a prime determining factor in Christian education. One of the commissions of the Study concentrated on curriculum. Its most significant finding was the statement of a new purpose and organizing principle for the curriculum:

> The purpose of the curriculum of Christian education is to
> confront individuals with the eternal gospel, and to nurture
> within them a life of faith, hope, and love in keeping with the
> gospel. The organizing principle of the curriculum from the
> viewpoint of the Christian gospel is to be found in the chang-
> ing needs and experiences of the individual as these include
> his relation to (1) God as revealed in Jesus Christ; (2) his
> fellow men and human society; (3) his place in the work of
> the world; (4) the Christian fellowship, the church; (5) the
> continuous process of history viewed as a carrier of the divine
> purpose and revealer of the moral law; (6) the universe in all
> its wonder and complexity.

This was an attempt to base curriculum upon a theologically
oriented purpose and an integral rather than merely selective
organizing principle, both Christian and educational at the
same time, giving ample emphasis to the experience of the
learner, the content of the Christian faith, and the demands of
the Christian life.

The current period is one of great ferment and creativity,
centered in the various denominations. The Presbyterian
Church in the U.S.A. launched its new curriculum, *Christian
Faith and Life: A Program for Church and Home,* in 1948. Of
its background, Park Hays Miller wrote:

> In 1941, a four-day conference was held in Atlantic City,
> attended by a cross section of the leadership of the church as
> well as by staff members. At this conference the members of
> the staff assumed the attitude of sponges with ears, receptive
> to the accumulated suggestions, criticisms, and desires of the
> representatives from the field. The suggestions were very valu-
> able, but it was felt that much more study was required to
> put them into operation.
>
> Therefore, another conference met for six weeks the following
> year, at Wagner College on Staten Island. More than forty
> carefully chosen delegates worshiped together and discussed
> their task with the utmost frankness and with a single purpose.

A new three-year cycle was planned, to provide a series of
lessons that would meet the needs of all the pupils as they ad-
vanced from year to year. It was the purpose of the course
to provide knowledge of the Bible as a whole, an understanding of the life and teachings of Jesus, and an appreciation
of the nature and work of the church, as they give meaning
and power to the Christian faith and life of children and young
people. (*Growing,* Oct.–Dec., 1948.)

James D. Smart assumed editorship of the new curriculum in
1944, and an editorial staff was at work on it by 1946. After
being introduced in a series of curriculum conferences and
training schools, it soon became widely accepted and approved.

When the Protestant Episcopal Church developed its Seabury Series, its serious and successful attempt was to make the
curriculum a thoroughly theological enterprise, even down to
the classroom methods utilized. Starting with an analysis of the
substance of the church's education in *The Church's Teaching
Series* (1949–1957), the editors went on to produce a closely
graded series (through the ninth grade) involving educational
encounter between the church, the teacher-observer team, and
the pupil group around the most acute problems of the pupil
and the community. An extremely flexible curriculum was
felt to be feasible because of the assumption of certain "fixed
points" in the church's educational life, such as the Bible,
The Book of Common Prayer, The Hymnal, and the church
year. Basic to the success of the Seabury Series in a local parish
are parent and adult Christian education, the family service,
and the parish-life conference. This last, the parish-life conference, is a workshop situation in which the purpose and work
of a parish are carefully analyzed in order to serve as background for deciding what is needed and appropriate by way of
Christian education.

Although no curriculum materials, as such, have been produced as yet, the "Long Range Program of Parish Education"
of four Lutheran bodies represents a new and promising approach to curriculum through painstaking research. The pur-

pose of the program is "to devise a master plan to guide the de-velopment of parish education for a decade or decades." The plan is to be accomplished in four phases: (1) the development of general and age group objectives for Christian education; (2) the development of a curriculum design; (3) the production of materials for instruction; (4) the introduction of the pro-gram into the congregations of the co-operating churches. After comprehensive preliminary studies, the first phase resulted in the publication of *The Objectives of Christian Education* (1957), a general statement of basic philosophy and goals, and *The Age-Level Objectives of Christian Education* (1958), a voluminous and meticulously compiled age-level calibration of the general objectives. At present the second phase of the program is being developed, two volumes having been pub-lished under the title *The Functional Objectives for Christian Education* (1959). The concern at this point in the program is for the very practical matter of "co-ordination of the efforts of the educational agencies of the congregation":

> In the past, agencies, such as the Sunday school, vacation church school, and weekday church school, have operated largely independently of one another and there has been little co-ordination among their curricula. Consequently the learner who was exposed to the program of a number of these agencies was likely to see very little relevance among his experience in them and may have encountered overlapping, repetition, or omissions. The curriculum design now underway is an attempt to effect unity in the total curriculum and to provide the learner with related experiences in all agencies.

> The present study has been limited to those agencies and programs considered basic to parish education in a well-organized congregation: the Christian family, Sunday school, vacation church school, weekday church school, catechetics, and leadership education. The procedures used in the study have included: first, an investigation of the nature of the learning process; second, a study of an organizing principle for cur-riculum to implement desired learnings; third, research on the

level of educational work in the co-operating bodies; fourth, a study of the potentialities and limitations of the existing parish education agencies and programs; fifth, development of general functional statements for each agency or program; and sixth, interpretation of the general functions of each agency or program at the various age levels where it is operative. (*The Functional Objectives for Christian Education*, Vol. I, p. 10.)

With the merger of the Congregational Christian Churches and the Evangelical and Reformed Church to form the United Church of Christ, a totally new curriculum is being developed, based upon commonly accepted theological and educational presuppositions, stated in *A Statement of Educational Principles as Seen in the Light of Christian Theology and Beliefs* (1957) and upon new analyses of the needs of persons at the various age and experience levels.

The Presbyterian Church in the U.S. has been engaged for several years in a "curriculum improvement program," out of which is likely to come a new curriculum. Basic curriculum principles were first stated in a working paper, *Christian Education Within the Covenant Community—the Church* (1958), as follows: the educational work of the church should be undertaken through a reverent study of the Bible; through the church, which is the family of God, as instrument of communication; with an understanding of the nature and need of man; with concern for the new life in Christ; and with methods that are in harmony with the nature of revelation. Intensive work in spelling out the implications of these principles for children's work, youth work, adult work, family life, and leadership education is being undertaken. At the same time a number of local churches, representative of various types of parishes and communities, are studying the principles with the co-operation of a research staff, seeking to draw out and design new plans and programs that will embody and express the principles under their particular circumstances.

With the production of a new curriculum already well along,

The United Church of Canada, after years of discussion that has engaged not only the Christian education staff but the whole denomination, is using the following organizing principle:

> The curriculum of Christian education may be organized by providing systematic opportunities for persons to be confronted with the gospel in the Christian community.
>
> Such organization will be concerned with the content, the process, and the setting of the curriculum.
>
> Our first concern is to present the gospel with integrity to children and adults at each age level. To do this means that God's revelation in Jesus Christ, God's revelation recorded in the Bible, and God's revelation proclaimed in the church will determine the content of the curriculum.
>
> Our second concern is that the varying abilities of the learners to appropriate the gospel will determine the process by which the content of the curriculum is presented.
>
> Our third concern is that the curriculum plan take into account the setting in which the curriculum is used. This includes the nature of the church as a teaching and worshipping fellowship, the organization of the local Sunday church school, and what is expected of the Sunday church school by the congregation and by the denomination. It also includes the nature of the family as a primary agency for Christian education. ("Curriculum: Its Organizing Principle, Plan, and Unit Descriptions," a working paper, July 3, 1959.)

Outside the denominations, but sometimes using the standard outlines, a number of commercial lesson series have been produced and marketed. In general, when the church makes a curriculum change a vacuum is created where that change is not accepted, a vacuum that commercial groups move in to fill.

For many years curriculum and lesson-planning was centered in interdenominational committees, first with the National Sunday School Convention, then with the International Council of Religious Education, and finally with the National Council of the Churches of Christ in the U.S.A. For some time, however, the curriculum committees of the National Council of Churches have been devoting considerable study to principles and procedures to serve as guides to the many curriculum enterprises being undertaken. In this way, it is likely that new and functional relationships will soon develop between the denominations and the interdenominational committees, reflecting a variety of needs and patterns rather than concentrating upon limited tasks.

Deeply influential in recent curriculum developments have been a number of volumes in Christian education, representing over the past fifteen years a new concern for theological and educational validity. Among the most influential are Paul H. Vieth's *The Church and Christian Education,* summarizing the Study of Christian Education; his *The Church School,* an excellent combination of the theoretical and the practical in parish education; Randolph Crump Miller's three books, *The Clue to Christian Education, Education for Christian Living,* and *Biblical Theology and Christian Education,* all of which include guidance on theology and the curriculum; James D. Smart's *The Teaching Ministry of the Church,* important in part because of Smart's connection with the Presbyterian (U.S.A.) curriculum but also because of his stature as an independent theoretician; Lewis Joseph Sherrill's *The Gift of Power* and *The Struggle of the Soul,* both of which plumb new depths of understanding of human need and the resources of the Christian faith to meet those needs; Howard Grimes's *The Church Redemptive,* which centers nurture in the community of faith; Reuel L. Howe's *Man's Need and God's Action,* where a "theology of relationships" is explored as a foundation for Christian education; Iris V. Cully's *The Dynamics of Christian Education,* a pioneering study of theology as a guide to Christian education method; and Allen O. Miller's *Invitation to Theology,* in which the task of the church in education is presented as theological in nature and involving lay people at the heart of the theological task.

Outside the church, in the general field of education, curriculum developments of great significance for the church have taken place. Representative of the creative work done are such books as Virgil E. Herrick and Ralph W. Tyler's *Toward Improved Curriculum Theory*, which states the basic curriculum issues with precision; Florence B. Stratemeyer (and others), *Developing a Curriculum for Modern Living*, in which the organizing principle of "persistent life situations" is thoroughly presented; Vernon E. Anderson's *Principles and Procedures of Curriculum Improvement*, exploring the curriculum as systematic problem-solving; Edward A. Krug's *Curriculum Planning*, summarizing in useful fashion the best current thinking on curriculum; and Daniel A. Prescott's *The Child in the Educative Process*, the most complete guide to individualizing the curriculum. History and research in curriculum have been dealt with in an article on curriculum by Nolan C. Kearney and Walter W. Cook, in the *Encyclopedia of Educational Research*, edited by Chester W. Harris.

As a mere hint at the educational trends that have challenged Christian education in the last decades such matters as testing and measurement, child development research, education for mental health, group methods, and audio-visuals might be mentioned. At a deeper level, the shift in philosophical emphasis from idealism and naturalism to pragmatism and realism has made it necessary for the church to re-examine its own theological and philosophical foundations for education. A short summary of *One Hundred Years of Curriculum Improvement, 1857–1957*, issued by the Association for Supervision and Curriculum Development of the National Education Association, cites the following significant changes in curriculum: change from faculty psychology of learning with emphasis upon memorization and mental discipline to an organismic, dynamic psychology with emphasis upon the powerful forces of purpose, meaning, goal-seeking, differentiation and integration in the learning process; change from reliance on tradition and subjective judgment as a basis for educational procedures to concern for scientific research and the application of scientific method and scientific findings; changes in methods and materials that have grown out of the idea that how we learn is as important as what we learn; and changes in patterns of participation, particularly teacher, teacher-pupil, and lay participation in curriculum building.

NATIONAL COUNCIL STUDIES

During the decade of the 1950's the National Council of the Churches of Christ in the U.S.A. has conducted a number of studies directly concerned with curriculum and a number of studies concerned with objectives in the curriculum. Studies of objectives are of importance for curriculum, since when objectives change, the curriculum changes.

Before the 1930's, Paul H. Vieth conducted his study of objectives, resulting in seven objectives identified by consensus. These objectives stressed the development of the person in relation to the great objects and concerns of faith. This approach reached its highest point in *Christian Education Today* (1940), where Vieth's seven objectives were expanded to eight and were stated officially as objectives of Christian education within the context of a basic philosophy. The focuses of the eight objectives were God, Jesus Christ, character, the social order, the church, the family, a philosophy of life, and the Bible. At this juncture, in the context developed for the objectives, the theological movement began to be significantly felt, although inner contradictions in point of view were not ironed out.

The theological movement, as has been pointed out, became dominant in the Study of Christian Education in the mid-1940's. However, the issuance of *Junior High Objectives* (1953) was the turning point so far as objectives are concerned. Here the objectives were stated in specifically theological categories, although the developmental character of the educational process was carefully safeguarded by attempting to state in each case where the person should be with regard to the objective upon entering the junior high years, where he should be upon leaving junior high, and the curriculum implications for the three-year process.

In 1952 a special committee on Christian education objectives was authorized. After extensive exploratory studies, the report *The Objectives of Christian Education* (1958) was issued, based upon the conviction that Christian education is one important phase of the church's mission. The "one objective" idea was linked to a more analytical statement of the concerns of Christian education in this way:

> The supreme purpose of Christian education is to enable persons to become aware of the seeking love of God as revealed in Jesus Christ and to respond in faith to his love in ways that will help them to grow as children of God, live in accordance with the will of God, and sustain a vital relationship to the Christian community.
>
> To achieve this purpose Christian education, under the guidance of the Holy Spirit, endeavors:
>
> To assist persons, at each stage of development, to realize the highest potentialities of the self as divinely created, to commit themselves to Christ, and to grow toward maturity as Christian persons;
>
> To help persons establish and maintain Christian relationships with their families, their churches, and with other individuals and groups, taking responsible roles in society, and seeing in every human being an object of the love of God;
>
> To aid persons in gaining a better understanding and awareness of the natural world as God's creation and accepting the responsibility for conserving its values and using them in the service of God and of mankind;
>
> To lead persons to an increasing understanding and appreciation of the Bible, whereby they may hear and obey the Word of God; to help them appreciate and use effectively other elements in the historic Christian heritage;
>
> To enable persons to discover and fulfill responsible roles in the Christian fellowship through faithful participation in the local and world mission of the church. (Pp. 21–22.)

The committee, in making its report, suggested that further study of educational and theological implications and formu-

lation of developmental goals and specific aims be undertaken.
When the work on junior high objectives was finished, interest turned to the senior high years. In the introduction to
its report, the committee on senior high objectives gives the
following account of its work:

> A growing concern for a more effective ministry to youth in
> current American culture led the Committee on Youth Work
> and the Committee on the Graded Series of the Division of
> Christian Education of the National Council of Churches to
> undertake this study jointly, through a committee composed
> of members of the two parent committees.
>
> This special committee held five meetings, each of approxi-
> mately one week, over a period of three years, beginning in
> November, 1954. Time between meetings was given to special
> assignments, consultation with associates, and review of the
> committee findings by the parent committee, Christian educa-
> tion staffs of co-operating denominations, and professors of
> Christian education. Throughout this period, the membership
> of the committee remained remarkably constant.
>
> The close and careful study of the senior high person, in
> the light of the implications of the gospel of Jesus Christ for
> him, led the committee to the conviction that there is one
> single objective rather than a list of objectives.

This committee, working with the concept of one objective,
developed a theory of Christian education as taking place
within an inclusive setting consisting of the world of persons
and the self, the family, the community, the larger society, the
natural world, history, and the church and the gospel. In this
setting, the objective of Christian education is

> to help persons to be aware of God's self-disclosure and
> seeking love in Jesus Christ and to respond in faith and love—
> to the end that they may know who they are and what their
> human situation means, grow as sons of God rooted in the
> Christian community, live in the Spirit of God in every rela-
> tionship, fulfill their common discipleship in the world, and
> abide in the Christian hope. (Pp. 14–15.)

The contribution of education to the achievement of this objective involves the undertaking of certain lifelong learning tasks: (1) listening with growing alertness to the gospel and responding in faith and love; (2) exploring the whole field of relationships in the light of the gospel; (3) discovering meaning and value in the field of relationships in the light of the gospel; (4) appropriating that meaning and value personally; (5) assuming personal and social responsibility in the light of the gospel. Some preliminary implications of this viewpoint for curriculum were hinted at:

> In curriculum the function of the objective is to inform and draw to itself every aspect of the curriculum, including every unit. The one objective is, therefore, the objective for every learning task, every lesson, every unit, every meeting throughout the whole curriculum. The curriculum's direction is determined by the one objective. Its plans are examined to see whether they are in harmony with and give promise of fostering progress toward the objective. Its results are evaluated in terms of their approximation to the objective. (P. 13.)

Reaping the harvest of psychology, theology, and education, the senior high committee thus came to the conviction that there is one objective for Christian education and that the one objective informs and guides in every situation and at every age level.

Both the senior high and general studies were authorized for publication by the National Council of Churches in 1958 as study papers. In the same action, the council requested that other age-level and curriculum committees proceed with further studies of objectives.

Following through on this action, study has been carried on by the children's workers looking to new insight in this field, the junior high area is being restudied, a special committee is pushing ahead on the whole question of youth curriculum and program, and adult workers have tackled the question. The adult workers began their study with a special workshop, held at the University of Pittsburgh in the summer of 1958, the proceedings of which have been published as *The Future Course of Christian Adult Education,* by Lawrence C. Little, editor.

Since 1957 the curriculum committees of the National Council of Churches have been engaged in a joint study, the purpose of which is to arrive at common understandings of the basic principles of curriculum building from which our denominations can develop materials for curriculum. The prime question is, "What kind of curriculum is needed by our churches in the task of Christian education?" This has become a concern not simply of editors but also of those who develop programs, administrators, those who produce materials, those in research and study, and those in charge of distribution. The main thrusts in Christian education in the recent past have come from the curriculum committees of the National Council of Churches. The Council has been a focal point, and a reflective screen, for the efforts of individual denominations, as well as a discovery arena for those denominations which are awakening to the need for a new approach to curriculum. The present volume seeks to make the findings of these studies available and to interpret them.

In the 1957 spring meeting, attention was given to theological foundations and psychological insights. The 1958 spring meeting centered upon the Bible in the curriculum and opened up the question of curriculum theory. Pursuing the matter of curriculum theory, the committee asked that a study paper be prepared for its 1958 winter meeting, dealing with the following questions: (1) How do you define certain terms that are essential to the task we have to perform? (2) What is the function of the objective (or objectives) of Christian education in curriculum? How shall the objective (or objectives) be used in curriculum building? (3) What should be the organizing principle for the curriculum? (4) What are the areas of Christian faith and life to be included in the curriculum? In this regard, what is the place of theology in the curriculum? (5) How would you develop the curriculum to provide for progression throughout? (6) How are comprehensiveness, sequence, balance, and flexibility to be achieved?

The study paper prepared in the light of this request sought to bring together the most significant and pertinent material from past meetings and from the various studies that had been undertaken, to draw implications from these materials, and to develop new ideas on the questions raised. The study paper was analyzed in detail by the committee, and key concepts reworked. The revisions thus arrived at were presented at the 1959 spring meetings.

Subsequent work has been done on the questions of theology, psychology, sequence, evaluation, and design. In this connection, specialists from the various fields have acted as continuing consultants to the committee. The study is likely to have a variety of practical results, one of which may be a new pattern of co-operative curriculum planning.

The questions with which all these studies are grappling are the major questions confronting Christian education today: (1) What is Christian education? (2) What is the aim of Christian education? (3) What constitutes the lifelong comprehensive curriculum? (4) What methods are appropriate? (5) What leadership is needed, and how shall it be trained? (6) How may our programs and institutions be restyled so as to be the church at work and worship? (7) How may Christian education be undergirded by a thoroughly theological and educational understanding?

These questions have grown out of the very difficult situation that Christian education has faced and is now facing, a situation of vast technological and cultural change. It is a situation in which the church is attempting rather desperately to make up its mind what it is, what it believes, and what it should be doing; one of changing educational ideals and patterns. Moreover, it is an educational situation in the United States (other countries having their own similar patterns and problems) that has pushed the Christian community into trying to provide education that consists of both supplementary training and basic orientation. The program of Christian education has tended to copy local educational styles and forms rather uncritically, allowing itself to grow in a haphazard fashion (sometimes bushy and overlapping, sometimes overextended and thin, with scarcely any attention to feeding, pruning, spacing, or balanced styling), lacking commonly shared understandings and theory, and lacking (until recently) support and supervision by the churches.

In the midst of these difficulties, there is the need for the most serious consideration of the questions that are troubling Christian education. This is what the denominations, the theorists, and the National Council of Churches are trying to do. What they are after is basic theory: objectives and principles that are adequate and sound, whose underlying assumptions are known and examined, and that will provide for them the guides that are needed for effective Christian education practice.

Is there a growing consensus? This is what is to be examined here in terms of the questions of context, scope, purpose, process, organizing principle, organizing medium, and design of the curriculum.

CURRENT DIRECTIONS

Christian education in America has come through a missionary phase, an educational phase, and a theological phase. The "curriculum" idea has replaced the "lesson series" idea. Various curriculums have been experimented with, stressing the Bible as content, the Bible applied to life, churchmanship, religious experience, social responsibility, and theology.

Christian education and its curriculum evidently respond to change in the world and the climate around it: changes in the national and international situation, the prevailing outlook of the people, philosophy, psychology and the other behavioral sciences, education, theology, and the way the church lives and does its work.

This is as it should be. Christian education is the church's concern for the person as he experiences and develops. Chief among its concerns, then, is the "live" communication of the Christian faith, a process of communicating that requires integrity and understandability on the part of the church and responsibility and appropriation on the part of the person. Unless Christian education and the church respond thus, they become more and more irrelevant.

What new factors are affecting us? First, a changing general outlook is having its effect. As important as any other aspects of this changed general outlook are the altered balance between national and international interests, the new images of man that are emerging, and the altered balance between the individual and the interpersonal, the latter becoming increasingly evident in theology, psychiatry, and social psychology.

Second, we are experiencing a change in the substance and role of theology. Great ecumenical councils deal with the most fundamental theological questions, stimulating world-wide interest in them. Barth, Buber, and Bonhoeffer are the men of the hour. Systematic theology gives way to existential concerns and to Biblical theology; theology resists the pressures of the religious revival, on the one hand, and the pressures of an era of domestic prosperity and international turmoil, on the other.

Theology seeks a substantial basis for ethics, spurred on by the urgency of such ethical issues as integration, war, delinquency, and the disintegration of the family. The meaning and practice of mission, evangelism, worship, vocation, and education are re-examined. A new doctrine of man results in a new idea of pupil and teacher. A changed Christology results in a new idea of the problem and aim of Christian education. A revived doctrine of the church results in a new idea of the context of Christian education, while it calls for an explicit theology of the parish, the ministry, and the laity.

The practical results of theological change include a new

sharpening of purpose reflected in the studies of Christian education objectives, an emphasis on adult education, a sense of need for a new balance in emphasis between the age levels so far as education is concerned, and a new (if still vague) way of thinking about education in the parish.

Third, ferment in psychology and the other behavioral sciences is being felt in education. With Freud and his followers have come new insights on personality. The great debate on learning continues. New "longitudinal" studies are changing the picture of human development. Communications is becoming a science closely related to motivation. Sociology and social psychology are introducing new ideas of the influence of the group in education.

All this is resulting in changing conceptions of education and nurture. What is the person's capacity to learn? The question suggests concern for the gifted, the handicapped, and the whole field of individual, community, and cultural differences. Heretofore unsuspected dimensions of characterology are brought into play. Grading, standardization, a flexible curriculum, lifelong education, and the child's right to learn are all involved.

What should the person learn? The swing to the "fundamentals," the tools of living, away from adjustment and social skills, is noticeable. The interest is in science at the expense of philosophy and the humanities. The current cry for "content" is reflected in Christian education in a demand for increased theological and Biblical content, while the vital role of theology and Bible as guides to process goes unrecognized.

Why does the person learn? The psychologists suggest a vast range of motivations and quarrel among themselves as to the function and strength of the motives each regards as central. David Riesman warns of inner-directedness and other-directedness, suggesting hesitatingly that there may be a possibility of autonomy. The emotional factors in learning are stressed to the exclusion of the rational processes of mind.

How does the person learn? The learning-theory debate, the progress of communications theory, and both the "longitudinal" and "horizontal" positions in developmental psychology have contributions to make to our understanding of how learning takes place. We know that learning takes place through perception, insight, and discrimination; through practice; through problem-solving; and through identification with a person, object, or cause. We know that method must be selected in accordance with purpose. We know that learning is at once social and personal and that shared developmental tasks and learning tasks are keys to profitable learning investment on the part of groups and individuals.

What is the context in which the person learns? The emphasis in the general field of education is on a broader concept of context than the school. The school is still a focal point in learning, but the home, the community, the group, and the media of mass communication are known to play influential roles. In the school itself, the place of "content" is being re-examined, flexible grading and individualization of the curriculum are being tried, new forms of unit organization are the subject of experimentation, and the role of the pupil in educational planning is being explored. The church is struggling with the concept of its role as the worshiping, witnessing, working community, and at the same time examining its policy of supplementary education. Both church and school are discovering that education depends both upon the context in which it takes place and upon the individual and corporate involvement in the very meaning and life that context represents. The attainment of a clearer conception and practice of educational evaluation in both settings awaits further and more mature experience with them and decision as to their meaning and significance.

Obviously, such changes as these in our general outlook, in theology, and in the behavioral sciences as they relate to education will make for changes in curriculum. Curriculum is seen as inclusive of more than the Sunday morning church school. The role of materials and the idea of "curriculum program" are being looked into carefully. The content or substance of the curriculum is being both enlarged and consolidated. New ways of teaching and learning are being sought. Thus the present concerns of Christian education curriculum include context, scope, purpose, process, organization, and design. Ways of attaining meaningful sequence, continuity, and progression are under investigation. The possibility of flexibility is being explored, flexibility of setting and method, in terms of individual, community, and cultural differences.

Some immediate questions present themselves. Shall Christian education seek more time? Shall a congregational approach, rather than a family or age-level approach, be given priority? Shall the types of materials issued be altered? What about changes in leadership education—in the very concept of leadership as vocation and discipleship, in providing less structured and more creative lesson and session plans, and in making parish, local, and regional supervision available? How may realism about Christian living be introduced into the curriculum? What policies shall govern the place and use of the Bible in the curriculum? How may the relation between the basic objective and specific aims and goals be established?

There are new convictions on these questions that are widely shared, yet are virtually untried. Most Christian educators are convinced that the Bible must be presented as the Word of God so that the pupil will know that it is intended to speak to him, sound scholarship and critical interpretation being combined with devout expectation. Most Christian educators are convinced that the reality of Jesus Christ as the incarnate God, the Savior, and the indwelling Redeemer must be presented so that the pupil will meet him, recognize him, give himself to him, and walk with him. Most Christian educators are convinced that the church must be presented as the most dynamic, living fellowship that the pupil encounters in his experience, its teachings to be taken utterly seriously. Most Christian educators are convinced that the pupil must be challenged to understand and accept his responsibilities for mission, social education and action, stewardship, and Christian family life.

How are we responding to these signs of the times? At least we are beginning to be aware of them, whether we meet them with resistance, accommodation, or creative change. Perhaps it is well that for the time being we may be plagued with a sense of failure (when we look at what we should be doing in study, creative expression, action, fellowship, stewardship, and worship), a feeling that we are not communicating (in the church, with the neighbors, and beyond our circle), and an awareness of the fact that we are not very relevant (to the modern world, to the modern mind, and to the modern soul). Perhaps it is necessary for us to recognize that ours is a period in which the chief need is for "settling down," using what we have and what we know to do a better job.

Chapter 3

THE QUESTION OF OBJECTIVES

T HE QUESTION of objectives has already proved to be an important one for curriculum. Studies of objectives turn out to be studies of curriculum or at least to have significance for curriculum development. The material in the preceding chapter is sufficient indication of this fact.

The history of the making of objectives in recent Protestant education has been traced in *The Gospel and Christian Education* (pp. 120–125), and in Lawrence C. Little's chapter, "The Objectives of Protestant Religious Education," in Taylor's *Religious Education: A Comprehensive Survey*. The purpose of the present chapter is not to review these materials but to raise and discuss the matter of the nature, relationships, and uses of objectives.

THE PERIL OF PROCEEDING WITHOUT AIMS

As Christian educators, we are teachers of the Christian faith, teachers in Christ's church. At the same time we are part of a culture and share the life of a total community. But at certain important points our faith and our culture are not in harmony with each other on the aims of human life. If our faith and our culture do not agree on the meaning of life, how can they agree on the aims of education?

Being a teacher in Christ's church and at the same time

sharing the life of the secular community, how can one perform his teaching function conscientiously and effectively unless he knows where he stands? This means having clearly defined aims for teaching, aims that guide at every point in what one tries to do and to accomplish.

The importance of clear aims for Christian teaching becomes evident when we reflect on what happens when we proceed without a clear consciousness of our purpose. The peril of proceeding without aims is that three things may happen.

We may do what we are told (by the curriculum materials in most cases) without questioning it. The danger is sometimes mitigated if the curriculum materials are good ones and if the teacher follows them conscientiously. But most aimless teachers are fairly careless in their use of even good curriculum materials. The result of doing merely what we are told is that we have no way of knowing when and where we have arrived. This is "treadmill" teaching.

Or we may do just what comes naturally. We teach what comes into our heads, try to keep the pupils entertained, or meander along the twisting paths of their shifting and unguided interests. The result of just doing what comes naturally is that the values that are achieved are purely accidental and are few and far between. This is wasteful teaching.

Or without intending to do so, we teach something other than Christianity. The form this usually takes is that we teach whatever doctrines happen to be popular at the time, simply assuming that they are Christian because they are high-sounding and because the right people are expounding them. (Sometimes we do find teachers, however, who are consciously riding some doctrinal hobby.) The result of teaching something other than Christianity, however well-meaning, is betrayal of the Christian faith and the church. This is treacherous teaching.

On the positive side, how do clear aims help us in our teaching? When we are planning, they help us to decide what to do. While we are teaching, they help us to keep on the track. When we are evaluating, they help us to judge the degree of our success or failure.

THE PROBLEM OF OBJECTIVES IN EDUCATION

In public education there is a deep concern for objectives and their use. Herrick and Tyler, in *Toward Improved Curriculum Theory,* state the problem, "There is a much more adequate theory of the use of objectives in the process of evaluation than of the use of objectives in the planning and organization of the learning experiences of the curriculum" (p. 118). Parenthetically, the reason for this may be in the behavioral strictures that are usually placed on the formulation of objectives.

Herrick and Tyler have keen insight into the simplicity of objectives when they are designed for use, and their uselessness when they are tied to cut-and-dried logic: "There is need for a study of the problem of how to relate objectives to the basic orientations of the curriculum on the one hand and to the centers that are used for organizing the instruction program on the other. Such an examination might reveal that the definition and use of objectives in curriculum is not a logically straightforward listing of operationally defined objectives, but is a process of keeping the organizing center of the curriculum in mind and then determining what directives this decision gives for the defining and use of instructional objectives" (pp. 118–119).

In place of uncritical acceptance of objectives, there is a healthy insistence upon their validation: "There is need for someone to show, in a way that any other curriculum worker could understand, exactly how objectives are derived from the bases of the society, human knowledge, and the individual to be educated. At present the scissors-and-paste method, counting frequencies of mention, or borrowing intact the pontifical pronouncements of learned committees are the most commonly used techniques for deriving the objectives to be used to give direction to America's schools. A worker in curriculum theory would throw away the first two as inadequate and test the third by challenging the learned committees to reveal the basis and techniques by which they arrived at their listing. Any statement of objectives should be able to stand an examination of its sources and procedures of derivation" (p. 119).

Types of Objectives in Christian Education

What types of objectives do we need in Christian education? Shall the objective be functional? That is, shall it stress some aspect or aspects of the service that Christian education should perform, such as mission? Shall it be psychological? That is, shall it stress what it should accomplish with the people Christian education serves: conversion or commitment, perhaps? Shall it be operational? That is, shall it stress some aspect or aspects of the techniques involved in carrying out Christian education, such as study or worship? Shall it be theological? That is, shall it stress its doctrinal orientation and aim? Shall it be otherwise content-centered? That is, shall it point up the teaching of Bible, history, morality, or some other body of knowledge or information? Or shall the objective of Christian education be a combination of these? They all appear to be more or less legitimate and important.

Another way of approaching the problem is to inquire whether we want an objective that indicates over-all policy and direction, or whether we want to develop objectives in terms of pupils' aims, the aims of the church (ecumenical, denominational, or local), the school's aims, the teacher's aims, the sexton's aims, or the curriculum writer's aims.

From the pupil's point of view there is a multiplicity of personal aims engendered by his needs. Religion comes into the picture for him when he becomes concerned with questions of identity, relationships, universal meaning, and purposes.

From the church's point of view, its mission and ministry determine its aim. However, since it is a church with a heritage, it expects that heritage to be taught, and since it is a living church with problems and a program, it expects enlistment and participation in its purposes, life, and work.

From the parents' or teacher's point of view the imperative to teach religion carries with it certain aims that he holds as an individual (like the evangelistic aim), and also certain aims (akin to those of the church) that he shares with other parents and teachers as a group.

One key problem, of course, is that of achieving shared aims, that is, aims that are mutually understood and accepted by pupil, church, parent, and teacher alike. The achievement of such shared aims is a prime responsibility of the curriculum.

Lest we delude ourselves that our problem of objectives is a recent one or easily disposed of, it is well for us to be reminded that Christian educators have struggled with the matter for a long time. For instance, B. S. Winchester was writing before 1915:

> Recent studies of (aims) maintain that the emphasis should be laid upon a few fundamental considerations, and that the criterion of judgment as to whether aims have been actually realized should be found in the activity or conduct of the pupil. . . .
>
> In order to standardize the educational processes, it is desirable that (the) fundamental factors be incorporated in a statement of the aims of education. These aims should be formulated, first, in terms of the life of the pupil, indicating with reference to each subject studied, and with reference to each successive period of development, just what is expected will take place in the pupil's life as a result of education, and as expressed in the pupil's conduct. Second, the aims should be formulated also in terms of the teacher's activity, showing clearly just what the teacher must do at each stage in the process in order to attain the aforesaid result in the pupil. Third, the aims need to be formulated in terms of school management, indicating again just what the administrative officers must do in order that the teachers may be able to realize through their teaching the results sought in the pupil. Similar formulation may be made to cover the larger aspects of organi-

zation including the training of teachers, the interrelating of educational agencies, and the selection and preparation of material. (*Encyclopedia of Sunday Schools and Religious Education*, p. 896.)

Archaic as Winchester's analysis proves to be, he is closer to solving the problem of objectives than many a contemporary theorist. He is at least willing to admit that an empirically derived typology of objectives would be of some help. This is precisely what is suggested in *The Objective of Christian Education for Senior High Young People* (pp. 11–13) and in *The Gospel and Christian Education* (pp. 114–120).

The term "objective" having been used in many different ways in educational literature and by educational theorists, it is important for our purposes to sort out the various meanings and to see how they are interrelated. The first issue is that of determining whether the problem of objectives is one for Christian education theory in general, thus calling primarily for one basic objective, or one for curriculum design in particular, thus calling for a variety of functional types of objectives. Resolve this confusion, and the matter becomes manageable.

What, then, are we after in objectives, guidance at the level of Christian education policy or guidance at the level of curriculum design? Depending on which is selected, how is it then proposed to solve the other set of problems? What form will the statement of objectives take? What substance will they contain? How is it proposed that they be used?

The solution proposed here, in the light of the National Council of Churches' studies thus far, is that a basic objective be established as the fundamental guide to policy, and that all other types of objectives be subordinated to it as they perform their proper functions in curriculum design.

The most complete typology of objectives available at present consists of the basic objective, personal ends, themes, topics and problems, group and individual goals, learning tasks, steps in developmental sequence, anticipated behavioral outcomes, and standards.

Basic objective. The basic objective is a statement of the purpose or basic function, the focus providing perspective, for the entire educational process. The conviction is growing that for this purpose one objective is needed, rather than lists of objectives or pyramids of objectives. One objective, in a comprehensive and meaningful setting, may be used in the broadest way to guide and evaluate curriculum plans and procedures. Three factors are seen to be interrelated: a setting for Christian education, an objective that guides work within the setting by indicating goals and aims, and routes (in harmony with the objective) through the setting by which the objective is reached. The basic objective is thus a policy statement intended as a guide for the whole Christian education process. "The objective's strength is in its drawing power—its ability to give unity, direction, and selectivity to the entire educational plan."

Any satisfactory statement of a basic objective must necessarily be similar to the purpose of the church, since they must be in accord with each other. A statement of the church's purpose, however, will stress mission and ministry while a statement of the purpose of Christian education will stress the ways in which the person and the group are fundamentally introduced to and inducted into that mission and ministry. What will be stressed then is awareness and response.

The existence and use of a basic objective does not eliminate the necessity for other types of objectives, such as those listed below. By itself, the basic objective cannot act as a tool for complete curriculum construction. The curriculum's direction is determined by the basic objective. Specific curriculum plans are examined to see whether they are in harmony with and give promise of fostering progress toward the objective. Results are evaluated in terms of their approximation to the objective. Here the themes, individual and group ends, unit topics and problems, teacher-pupil goals, and steps in developmental sequence are all seen and examined in light of the basic objective. But "in curriculum design no attempt should be made to have the suggested teacher-pupil goals add up cumulatively to the achievement of the single objective, nor should they be derived by segmenting the objective. The sum of these goals, themes, personal ends, topics, or problems does not equal the objectives. Rather, they are all seen and examined in the light of the objective." (*The Objective of Christian Education for Senior High Young People*, p. 13.)

Personal ends. The situation, needs, interests, concerns, and duties of the pupil and the group shape or constitute objectives for them. The personal and group objectives that are forthcoming are of the utmost significance because they are the only objectives that are really ever accomplished. In a sense, then, Christian education's task is that of the reconstruction and transformation of personal and group ends. A realistic curriculum takes this into account at every point.

Themes. Most often the objectives of Christian education have been stated in terms of the great concerns of the Christian faith and the Christian life. Such objectives, for all that they prefix such phrases as "to help pupils know," or "to develop in growing persons," actually constitute analyses of curriculum content or scope. Sometimes useful as statements of scope, such statements fail at two points: (1) They are too detailed to focus the objective of Christian education sharply. (2) They are often too brief to do justice to the range of relationships involved in a way that is really helpful for direction in curriculum building.

Topics and problems. Topics and problems represent specific adaptations of themes for purposes of curriculum construction. A great theme cannot be handled all at once in one piece. Within it topical focuses must be discovered, representative and sequential in nature. As these topics are dealt with, the theme (the great concern) is also dealt with. A problem is a topic encountered, which accounts for the educational power of a problem. For instance, within the great theme of the church, monasticism is a topic. But when I am challenged, "Why don't you become a monk?" the topic turns into a problem through personal encounter, and thus gains considerable educational strength.

Group and individual goals. Sometimes known as classroom goals, unit aims, or lesson aims, these group and individual goals come into existence when teacher and pupils make plans involving specific learning tasks (sometimes together, but often unfortunately in an un-co-ordinated way), carry out the plans, review, evaluate, and set new goals. Thus they are used by the teacher, leader, group, and individual pupil in working out particular units, lessons, meetings, or projects.

Because they are guides to a dynamic process, such goals tend to be fluid rather than rigid, making it difficult to anticipate them in a standard way. They are set up by a working group and guide its specific activities. Often educators, parents, pupils, and other members of the church and community may participate in formulating and reformulating them. Children, youth, and adults alike need practice in goal-setting and evaluation of individual and group development toward recognized and accepted goals.

Group and individual goals are used to guide a lesson, a unit, a year's work, a cycle; they give hints on procedure, keep the process on the track, and provide standards for evaluation; they are specific, detailed, simple, unitary, and cumulative.

How are such goals come by? Fundamentally we relate what is to be learned or gained to the developing stream of experience in light of the basic objective. This means: (1) Canvassing the areas of experience (themes) to be included in the content, seeing them logically, in order that they may be interpreted and ordered psychologically. (2) Canvassing the nature and needs of the learners involved. Here they are brought into the situation as active contributors. The curriculum planner, editor, or writer usually has to content himself with a cross-sectional sample, but the local leader has the advantage of

being able to enlist the group in the process. (3) Hypothesizing
the goals required. If the leader does this himself, adopts some
other group's formulation, or has a committee do it, then the
group, or a representative cross section of those for whom
the goals are intended, ought to be given the opportunity to
validate or revise the hypothesized goals. Obviously, specific
and detailed aims are always anchored in the general objective
but are relative to the themes on the one hand and to the
situations in which they are used on the other. Thus they
have unity and consistency but are subject to revision and
change.

The role of group and individual goals has been carefully
and systematically delineated in *The Objective of Christian
Education for Senior High Young People:*

> In organizing, selecting, and arranging its learning activities,
> a learning group would usually follow this procedure:
> —Discern the area to be explored (a theme, topic, or problem).
> —Set goals that anticipate listening to and responding to the
> gospel in the discovery and personal appropriation of meaning
> and value.
> —Make plans for specific learning activities involving ex-
> ploration, discovery of meaning and value, their personal ap-
> propriation, and the assumption of responsibility (if this last
> can be anticipated in specific terms).
> —Carry the plans through, alert to the possibility of the
> emergence of new experiences that have not yet been antici-
> pated that may call for different plans and procedures.
> —Weigh the results and determine their implications for
> responsible action.
> —Plan for and carry out the appropriate action, discern new
> areas to be explored, and set new goals accordingly. (Pp. 37–
> 38.)

Teaching-learning units will be much more valuable if they
will suggest *a range of goals* (all possible avenues toward the
objective) from which particular groups and individuals may

choose the one or more that may be most appropriate to their situation.

Group and individual goals are crucial in curriculum since within themselves they combine what is to be learned and also the force of personal motivation. If personal ends are the only objectives that are ever really achieved, the construction and reconstruction of group and individual goals provides the means by which motivations may become integrally related to the ends of Christian education. This is why the curriculum is designed in terms of themes involving the great realities of the Christian faith and concerns of the Christian life, interpreted as topics and problems, and at the same time designed in terms of the learning process, involving the co-operative setting of goals, engagement in activities appropriate to the accomplishment of those goals, and evaluation of the degree to which they are achieved.

Learning tasks. Learning tasks are the great general activities engaged in in the learning process. In many respects group and individual goals and learning tasks are the same thing. Yet it has been discovered that there is value in understanding that the group and individual goals of Christian education, the very specific learning tasks of Christian education, group themselves in five major categories that have come to be identified as the learning tasks of Christian education:

Listening with growing alertness to the gospel and responding in faith and love.

Exploring the whole field of relationships in the light of the gospel.

Discovering meaning and value in the field of relationships in the light of the gospel.

Appropriating that meaning and value personally.

Assuming personal and social responsibility in the light of the gospel.

Insight on the matter of learning tasks in Christian education has been gained from the attempt to use the concept of developmental tasks, as propounded by Robert J. Havighurst in *Human Development and Education*. Havighurst's theory of developmental tasks is that there are tasks to be undertaken at each stage of a person's development. If he undertakes them and succeeds with them, he grows and is ready for the next stage. If he does not, his growth is held back. The educator's chief responsibility in this regard is to help the individual to undertake tasks that are appropriate to him and to help him to succeed with them. The "tasks" idea has proved to be extremely useful and adaptable to Christian education, even though the developmental aspect of the concept has required modification. The learning tasks are conceived as lifelong tasks involving sequences of specific tasks or goals, a concept more germane to Christian education than that of task or goal clusters at various developmental levels.

Steps in developmental sequence. Steps in developmental sequence are calibrated levels of progress. The concept is intended to be substituted for that of "age-level objectives." Educational literature is replete with attempts to formulate goals in terms of developmental tasks for various age levels. Major attention has been given by committees of the National Council of Churches and by all curriculum people to the matter of "age-level objectives" as the basis for curriculum construction. Closely graded and group-graded materials have been based on the premise of the appropriateness of such objectives.

The level of progress at any time in the learning process is (1) the status of the situation, needs, and duties of the pupil or the group and (2) the status of the pupil's or the group's goals. In spite of the fact that these are often generalized into "age-level objectives," it is very deceptive to use them in this way.

The fundamental fact with which we deal in education is individual differences. "Age-level objectives" almost invariably

are built on the extremely dangerous assumption that an
average is an end. The false assumption is that rates of progress
are, or should be, uniform in sequences of experiences involved
in coming to grips with the great themes of the Christian faith
and the Christian life.

Such objectives might better be recognized for what they
are: points on a sequential scale of achievement, to which
the idea of "age levels" may very well be irrelevant in most
instances. Furthermore, they should be recognized as mainly
useful as evaluative indicators with individuals and groups.
Their usefulness in planning, however, is distinctly limited.
They may be helpful in determining teacher-pupil goals
within a given unit; they may even give the curriculum
planner some general notion of areas to be covered and experiences to be suggested at various times. But they are not
helpful at all in determining over-all curricular policy.

How shall useful calibrations of steps in developmental
sequence be set up? The suggestion is that this be done in
terms of the five great learning tasks. The individual and the
group use goals and activities in sequence in exploring, discovering meaning and value, and appropriating that meaning
and value personally as they encounter various aspects of the
field of their relationships. This is true of their experience in
the Christian faith and life, so that it may be said that "listening with growing alertness to the gospel and responding in
faith and love" itself involves exploration, discovery of meaning and value, and personal appropriation of that meaning
and value in sequential ways. There are undergirding sequences of assumption of personal and social responsibility
that flow from and feed into the other learning tasks. The possibility of a plurality of sequences is a very real one, since no
attempt at standardization of Christian experience in educational terms has ever been convincing or accepted.

Anticipated behavioral outcomes. Anticipated behavioral
outcomes are specific knowledges, skills, and attitudes expected
to result from the educational process. Much of the interest in

anticipated behavioral outcomes stems from the fact that educators generally feel that they are indispensable in evaluation. Two of the outstanding books in the field, Nolan C. Kearney's *Elementary School Objectives* and Will French's *Behavioral Goals of General Education in High School,* advocate primary attention to such objectives and tend to disparage the usefulness of other types. Elizabeth Hagen, in her contribution to *Evaluation and Christian Education,* conceives of the behavioral outcomes as basic to the whole process of curriculum: "The behavioral changes that we want to effect through our educational program provide the framework for building the curriculum for the program and selecting the learning experiences and teaching methods for the program. The curriculum, learning activities, and methods are means to an end—not an end in and of themselves" (p. 29). According to this position, planning and evaluation both depend upon concrete statements of desired behavioral outcomes. In order to evaluate, "one must know the objectives of the educational program not only in a general way but more importantly in terms of the changes in behavior that we want to produce. Although explicit statements of objectives are absolutely necessary for evaluation, one should not assume that they are not necessary before evaluation takes place. Objectives of an educational program provide the base for building the curriculum of the program as well as for the evaluation of the program" (p. 35).

This viewpoint needs to be seriously challenged at several points. Anticipated behavioral outcomes cannot be used systematically in constructing the program of Christian education and its curriculum. Although the outcomes of Christian education are behavioral, they cannot be anticipated in a standard way. Christian education is relational, not behavioristic; bringing man into encounter with God, his world, his fellow man, and himself will have behavioral results that may be anticipated in a general way (in terms of awareness and response, for instance) but that cannot be nailed down specifically in advance. Theologically, the relation of law and grace, and works and faith, is most pertinent here.

Although anticipated behavioral outcomes cannot determine the curriculum, they may serve a useful purpose in suggesting (not determining) possible topics and problems and group and individual goals. Furthermore, they will be useful in evaluation, not as standards to be applied in a rigid way but as clues to what is taking place in the development of the individual and the group. Thus serious attention to knowledges and understandings, attitudes, and action patterns related to the great concerns in terms of the accomplishment of the Christian learning tasks is merited if used with proper caution.

Standards. Winchester was calling for standards when he asked for formulation of aims in terms of school management and in terms of "the larger aspects of organization." Although not of the most direct concern to curriculum theory and design, standards must be included in any typology of educational objectives.

The purpose of developing this typology of objectives is not the establishment of a terminological pattern but rather the definition of the uses characteristically made of objectives in Christian education. If studies of objectives are to continue in Protestant education, as they undoubtedly will, it may be useful for those conducting such studies to have such a typology to sort out the various kinds of educational functions with which they are dealing.

CURRENT PROTESTANT EDUCATIONAL OBJECTIVES ANALYZED

Having established a typology of Christian education objectives, it may be put to use in the analysis of various denominational and interdenominational statements of objectives. The recent statements of the National Council of Churches will be analyzed first.

Junior High Objectives (1953) emphasizes themes (God, Jesus Christ, man, the social order, the church, and the Bible).

These themes are broken down into topics and problems. A junior high cross section of steps in developmental sequence ("incoming twelve-year-olds" and "desired outcomes") is provided, which could also be taken as an analysis of anticipated behavioral outcomes for juniors and junior highs. A variety of group and individual goals associated with the topics and problems ("implications") is suggested. A section on "Junior High Experiences" deals with personal ends. An "Introduction" suggests that the objective of Christian education is the church's mission to continue its teaching of the gospel of Jesus Christ in a rapidly changing world.

The Objectives of Christian Education (1958) discusses the problems that led to a new statement of objectives, and the way such statement was to be formulated. Further follow-up steps are outlined, including the study of educational and theological implications, the formulation of developmental goals, and the determination of specific aims. The aims and processes of Christian education are related to those of public education; their respective spheres of operation and their common responsibilities are analyzed. The document roots its analysis of objectives in a statement of the nature and mission of the church; a definition of Christian education; and a discussion of the relation of Christian education to the total task of the church, including a concept of the "maturing" Christian that grows out of a consensus regarding the essentials of the Christian faith, the essential elements of Christian growth, and the proper relation that these sustain to one another. Something of an outline of learning tasks is provided in a list of the characteristics and activities of the "maturing" Christian (p. 11). A "supreme purpose," analogous to a basic objective, is emphasized (p. 11). A list of themes is provided (Christian self-realization and personal maturity, social relationships, the natural world and the conservation of its values, the Bible and the Christian heritage, and responsible churchmanship). The unity of the themes under the supreme purpose is stressed.

The Objective of Christian Education for Senior High Young People (1958) emphasizes the basic objective and makes it the key to the whole process. An analysis of personal ends is provided in a section "Who Is the Senior High?" Themes are analyzed in terms of "The World the Senior High Lives In" (the field of relationships), as follows: personality (the world of persons and the self), the family, the community, the world (the larger society), the natural world, history, and the church and the gospel. An extensive analysis of the learning tasks that may be undertaken to reach the objective is given, showing in detail what is involved in undertaking these tasks. Topics and problems, and group and individual goals, are dealt with by outlining briefly the procedure a learning group uses in connection with following out the learning tasks (pp. 37–38), and by listing the responsibilities to be undertaken by various agencies (pp. 39–42). A clue to steps in developmental sequence is provided by an analysis of the sequences of activities involved with each learning task, by an indication of the sequential relationships among the various tasks (pp. 36–37, and chart), and by the provision of a brief "interpretation for senior highs" in connection with each task. Anticipated behavioral outcomes are interpreted only in general terms related directly to the basic objective.

Approaches to objectives in selected current statements by denominations are also illuminating on the various kinds of objectives employed, and the ways in which they may be related to each other as bases for curriculum.

The United Presbyterian statements are found in *Basic Principles* (1947) and *Christian Faith and Life at a Glance* (Revised, 1958). The communication of revelation by the church to the end of discipleship, in terms of the learner and his situation, is the key to Christian education. Three themes (the Lord of Christian faith and life, the Bible in Christian faith and life, and the church in Christian faith and life) are to be organized in terms of training for active discipleship. Church, church school, and home are all to be involved. Topics and problems, group and individual goals, steps in developmental sequence, and anticipated behavioral outcomes are all worked out in detail in terms of each of the three themes.

The Protestant Episcopal Church has produced *The Church's Teaching Series* (1949–1957) in six volumes: *The Holy Scriptures, Chapters in Church History, The Faith of the Church, The Worship of the Church, Christian Living,* and *The Episcopal Church and Its Work.* Much basic information is also contained in its annual *Preview,* the 1958–1959 issue being used in this analysis. Themes are established in the basic volumes, but they are used in a way that is always closely related to the personal ends of the pupil, relating the themes (the faith and heritage of the church) directly to the daily lives of children and adults. "The Christian revelation is not a message about God; it is God himself who 'for us men and our salvation' came among us. Growth in knowledge of this revelation, then, is not only education in the facts of our Christian heritage but also a living knowledge, a faith-full response to God." Recognizing the demands of subject matter and the readiness of the learner, a realistic approach to sequence is made in terms of the uniqueness of Christian experience: "We are never too young or too old to be nurtured in the Christian faith, and there is nothing that we more deeply need at every age. The subject we teach is always the same, and it is our job, as Christian educators, to reach our *children* in terms simple enough, and *adults* in terms of sufficient maturity, to evoke their meaningful response."

The Methodist statement is *Foundations of Christian Teaching in Methodist Churches* (1960). Christian education is a ministry of the church in a contemporary setting. The gospel the church teaches includes the Christian understanding of God and man, the character of God's work, man's response to God, the Christian hope, the Kingdom of God, and the Christian understanding of the Bible. The basic objective is: "Through Christian education the fellowship of believers (the church) seeks to help persons become aware of God's seeking

love as shown especially in Jesus Christ and to respond in
faith and love to the end that they may develop self-
understanding, self-acceptance, and self-fulfillment under God;
increasingly identify themselves as sons of God and members of
the Christian community; live as Christian disciples in all
relations in human society; and abide in the Christian hope."

Four Lutheran bodies have together produced *The Objectives of Christian Education* (1957), *Age-Level Objectives
of Christian Education* (1958), and *The Functional Objectives for Christian Education* (1959). One central objective
("to assist the individual in his response and witness to the
eternal and incarnate Word of God as he grows within this
community of the church toward greater maturity in his
Christian life through ever-deepening understandings, more
wholesome attitudes, and more responsible patterns of action")
is worked out in terms of six themes (God, the Christian
church, the Bible, the pupil's fellow men, the physical world,
and the pupil himself). These are developed, in turn, into
detailed listings of understandings, attitudes, and action patterns for each age group. Recognizing that the process of
Christian education must be directly related to the learner's
"continual life involvements," "continual Christian learnings" are analyzed. These are in the form of what we have
called learning tasks: continual Christian learnings in relation
to continual life involvements of a personal nature (personal
identity, "givenness" of life, confronting ultimate reality); in
relation to continual life involvements of an interpersonal
nature (with individuals, with "face-to-face" groups); in relation to continual life involvements of an impersonal nature
(physical world, economic structures and forces, political and
social structures and influences, religious traditions and influences). The continual Christian learnings listed under these
headings are then broken down into the way in which the
family, Sunday school, vacation school, weekday school, and
catechetics may serve most effectively at various age levels.

The Presbyterian Church in the U.S., in its *Christian*

Education Within the Covenant Community—the Church (1958), generally does not stress themes but processes and relationships. Thus "the educational work of the church is based upon the fact that God enters into covenant with his people, giving them a foundation of security out of which grows freedom to respond in maturity to the will of God. The covenant community is the visible manifestation of the redeemed family into which God is inviting all mankind, and it issues his invitation to men to be joined in covenant relationships with him through Jesus Christ. . . . The very life of the church is an educational experience. The church provides planned educational experiences in such activities as worship, preaching, teaching, counseling, and service." This means that the educational work of the church should be undertaken through a reverent study of the Bible; through the church, which is the family of God, as the instrument of communication; with an understanding of the nature and need of man; with concern for the character of the new life in Christ; and with methods that are in harmony with the nature of revelation.

In the statement of the United Church of Christ, *A Statement of Educational Principles as Seen in the Light of Christian Theology and Beliefs* (1957), themes (God, man, Jesus Christ, the Holy Spirit) are used in two ways: as an essential part of the content of Christian education and as sources for the basic implications for the nature of Christian education. These educational implications are drawn together in terms of teaching, learning, and the educational situation. Special attention is given to the Bible and its use. A basic objective is indicated in the statement, "The function of Christian education is to surround individuals with the reality of the Christian fellowship, past and present, so that they will respond in a free and responsible relationship to God and will become active participants in the Christian fellowship." Sequence is anticipated in terms of a continuum of experience through which "each growing person can identify himself with the fellowship and share its purposes, its worship, its beliefs, its work, and the fruits of the Spirit which it seeks to foster and support."

"The Great Objective" of the American Baptists is "the new person in Christ." Themes are expressed in the statement in terms of "basic realities revealed in the Bible": the divine origin of man, the tragedy of sin, the grace of God, the redemptive love of God in Jesus his Son, the Lordship of Christ, the re-creative power of the Holy Spirit, the unique life and mission of the church, the coming of the Kingdom of God, and the blessings of life eternal. Christian education materials and methods should be such as God may use, lead to conversion, and "seek to lead each person to grow in a life surrendered to Jesus Christ, to share in the redemptive fellowship of the church, to seek the will of God in all human relationships, and to participate in the work of Christ in evangelizing the home, the community, and the world."

The United Church of Canada developed its first booklet, *Presuppositions,* during the heat of the National Council studies. The curriculum themes were decided on during the time that the present volume was being written. The objective is: "That persons at each stage of their lives may know God, as he is revealed in Jesus Christ, and serve him in love through the worship, work, fellowship and witness of the church in the daily life of the world." Each of the themes implied in the objective is expressed as doctrinal affirmation plus a life-process concept: God and his purpose, Jesus Christ and the Christian life, the church and the world.

WHERE WE STAND ON OBJECTIVES

Some general conclusions may now be drawn from these studies of objectives. What is meant by "objectives" is being clarified. The sorting out and classification of the various things that the churches and schools mean when they use the term "objectives" suggests solutions to certain key problems.

We have hit upon a key idea in Christian education theory when we see objectives as "the objective of Christian education." This gives us as our objective one unified policy statement that indicates the whole intent of Christian education. Most of the recent statements have tended in this direction, out of necessity for such a guide to their work as it develops.

This, however, forces a rethinking of our ideas on sequence, for we seem to be moving away from age group categories. Even those who are developing age-level patterns as basic to their curriculums are using them in a far from static way. It may be predicted that curriculum people will have more and more difficulty with the concept of "age-level objectives." Some real help at this point may be forthcoming from the studies of Christian growth and the longitudinal developmental studies, but these have not yet been assimilated into our thinking and planning. Facing this problem in all its aspects may help us to discover many of the new ideas on curriculum design and the organization of our program that we need.

The "one objective" idea also forces a rethinking of what is to be learned in Christian education. The statement of objectives as themes, which has been customary heretofore, seemed to suggest various answers to the question of curriculum content but did not get to the "point" of Christian education. Now we can see clearly what we are looking for when we discuss this matter—not objectives, but "scope." The idea of the "field of relationships in the light of the gospel," appears to hold particular promise, especially because it is defensible in terms of theology, philosophy, and the behavioral sciences. Furthermore, these disciplines can provide great help on what makes up the field of relationships and what it means to experience it in the light of the gospel. Here most of the studies of objectives will have contributions to make, for this appears to be one of the distinctly open questions in Christian education. Once there is some agreement at this point there will be some possibility of stability in our analyses of "topics and problems." Agreement on themes will also provide guidance that we need on the development and selection of group and individual goals.

The other factor that has to be taken into account in developing and selecting group and individual goals, however, is personal ends. This has been only cursorily explored in our studies. Yet, because of their power to get things accomplished, this is the most important area of all. Until, for instance, the person becomes motivated "to be aware of the gospel and to respond in faith and love," nothing really significant is achieved. "Helping persons" to such awareness and response is a matter of stimulating and guiding them in changing and developing their personal ends, as well as in working them out. The problem of group motivation will be helped toward solution by the use of a single objective. Its use will encourage individuals and groups to set their own goals for learning in harmony with it. Their learning will thus be motivated because they are working toward their own chosen goals, and the old question, "How shall we get the group interested in pursuing the curriculum's goals?" will be eliminated.

The secret of Christian education practice may be in the development and use of group and individual goals that will link together in a vital way personal ends and the great concerns of the Christian faith and the Christian life (probably via topics and problems), held together and focused by the basic objective. If this be true, then one might proceed on the principle that these group and individual goals will be specific aspects of the learning tasks of Christian education.

The learning tasks appear to offer invaluable assistance in tying together in an experience process that is essentially personal, and thus interpersonal, the learning tasks of the individual and the group and the great concerns of the Christian faith and life. This may be the clue, as a matter of fact, to the whole problem of curriculum and administration, since curriculum may be thought of as the design and direction of the learning tasks, and administration may be thought of as providing the organizational, managerial, and supervisory implementation for them.

"Anticipated behavioral outcomes" become less a focus of attention in Christian education because a great variety of valid and appropriate response is possible, and standardization of response has its obvious dangers. Analysis of standard responses is useful in estimating where a person is or what a group's next steps may be but must be used with the utmost caution. In planning curriculum and program such analyses may be used to suggest possibilities but never to freeze patterns. Our stalemate in Christian education evaluation is due to our trying to derive curriculum from general objectives that were unrealistic because they could not apply to many local situations. One well understood and generally accepted objective, in terms of which direction may be sighted and a course charted in any curriculum situation, will help us to re-establish a basis for evaluation. It will help because its use will be correlated with the necessity for setting instructional goals cooperatively on the local level. Such goals may serve not only for evaluation of results by teachers but may also serve for individual and group self-evaluation.

The chief findings of the studies might, then, be summarized in terms of the context, scope, purpose, process, and design of Christian education. There appears to be something of a growing consensus on these matters. The context of Christian education is seen as the worshiping, witnessing, working community of persons in Christ. The scope of Christian education is the whole field of relationships in the light of the gospel. The purpose of Christian education is awareness of revelation and the gospel, and response in faith and love. The process of Christian education is participation in the life and work of the community of persons in Christ. The design of Christian education consists of sequences of activities and experiences by which the learning tasks may be effectively undertaken by individuals and groups. This apparent consensus is explored in Part II.

PART
II

Theory

PART
II

Theory

Theory...

CURRICULUM THEORY CONSISTS OF THE PRINCIPLES THAT ACT AS sound guides to curriculum practice: principles with respect to the orientation of the curriculum, the design of the curriculum, and the use and evaluation of the curriculum. The construction of curriculum theory in Christian education involves knowing the curriculum task, asking the right questions, marshaling the needed resources and help, and formulating the required principles.

A principle is a statement of a dependable relationship between two or more variables. Christian education principles are statements of dependable relationships involving the culture, the individual, Christianity, and education. Such principles are derived from theology, the church's life and work, the philosophical and historical disciplines, from the behavioral sciences, and from the study of communication. In other words, a comprehensive set of the sources of the most dependable and pertinent information is used in the formation of principles of Christian education.

In order to get the needed principles, however, Christian educators must seek information from these sources by asking the right questions. Only as the questions are clear and accurately stated may useful answers be given. Six such questions are proposed as the basis for fundamental curriculum understandings:

Where is the curriculum? What is the locus of the curriculum of Christian education? Where does Christian education's communicative transaction really take place? This is the question of the context of Christian education.

What is in the curriculum? What is the curriculum's substance? What does it have to communicate? This is the question of the scope of Christian education and its curriculum.

Why is the curriculum? What is its objective? This is the question of the purpose of Christian education and its curriculum.

How is the curriculum? How does the communicative transaction take place in Christian education? What is the clue to process and method? This is the question of the process of Christian education and its curriculum.

In what way shall the curriculum be organized? How shall all pertinent factors be taken into account, weighed, and related to one another in such a way that the practicalities of a curriculum organized for use may be achieved? This is the question of the organizing principle of the curriculum.

By what means shall the curriculum be organized? What instrumentalities are available, in harmony with the organizing principle, by which the curriculum may be worked out in practice? This is the question of the organizing medium for the curriculum.

Curriculum issues have not always been stated clearly and systematically, making it exceedingly difficult to inquire intelligently of the basic disciplines for the help they might have to offer. Furthermore, these foundation disciplines have not, in the main, been designed to be of help to education; this has not been their function or intention. Among themselves they do not always speak completely, clearly, or consistently. Education and Christian education, just beginning to discover how to organize and use what the foundation disciplines have to offer, have a long and difficult task ahead. The length and difficulty of the road ahead is fully reflected in the pages that follow.

Curriculum principles, in the manner of other principles of Christian education, are to be used as dependable guides to practice. They need to be tested by reference back to the sources and foundation disciplines on the one hand and by the degree to which they operate satisfactorily in practice on the other. The problem of validating curriculum principles involves determining their appropriateness, their adequacy, and their utility. Such questions as the following must be answered to determine the validity of any principles proposed:

Are they relevant to the problems they are intended to solve?

Are they adequate to the task required of them?

Are they effective in dealing with the problems for which they are intended?

Are they checked continually for theoretical adequacy and soundness?

Are they accepted in the appropriate quarters?

Are they used in the appropriate quarters?

All of us have questions in our minds about what we do when we teach. Are we doing the best things? Could we do better teaching if we did it differently? And we have questions in our minds about what we are trying to get across. Are we making God's will really clear? Are we teaching the whole gospel as it should be taught? Are we getting across who Jesus Christ really was, and who he is?

These are hard questions to answer, and there are many more like them. When we ask them and try to think of answers, we are trying to understand what we are doing. We are "theorizing" about what we are doing as Christian educators. The questions we ask when we are trying to understand what we are doing and the answers we give to those questions are our "curriculum theory."

Every Christian educator has a curriculum theory, whether he knows it or not, because no one can be a Christian teacher without trying to understand what he is doing. But it is true also that there is no Christian teacher who could not benefit from having his curriculum theory looked into and improved. What we are really doing in curriculum theory is to look at our work as Christian teachers, ask every question we can about it to try to understand it, and seek ways of improving what we are doing. This is done with the conviction that we will do a better job in Christian education curriculum if we see Christian education in its setting, if we know what we are doing and why we are doing it, and if we select our materials and methods with a full knowledge of what is available to us.

Chapter 4

BASING THE CURRICULUM
ON SOUND PRINCIPLES

T HE CURRICULUM should be a rich and dependable resource, a reliable tool in the hands of teachers and learners, helping them to accomplish their purposes in Christian education. As soon as the question of goals and how we reach them is raised, we find ourselves turning to theology, philosophy, history, psychology, sociology, and communications for answers.

Why? Because these are the means that have been given to us, or that we have devised, for understanding life and existence. These disciplines focus upon the questions of what life is, what it means, and how to live it. Since education is the chief way in which life is guided, transformed, and reconstructed, the understandings we get from these sources and disciplines become its foundations. Thus the principles we use to plan the curriculum, among other educational enterprises, must be based upon the best understandings we can achieve from the foundation disciplines.

FOUNDATIONS AND THEIR USES

For education, the foundation disciplines come to a point in theory, because theory consists of sound guides to practice. Christian education is a practical matter, a way of getting

something done that needs doing. Christian education's work
is its ministry to children, youth, adults, families, congregations, communities, and society. It finds itself in serving them.
Primarily, it seeks to minister to "the life of man in the light
of God." The ministry that Christian education seeks to perform may be symbolized by saying that it is to assist in
enabling men to meet, know, love, and serve Jesus Christ.

Immediately it becomes evident, in the light of such a
ministry, that Christian education must be clear on such questions as: Who is Jesus Christ? What is man—his nature, his
situation, his destiny? How can the individual be interpreted
in terms of "man"? What is mankind? What is human "becoming"? How does it take place? Can it be guided? How?

These questions and others like them, once raised, call for
the best answers available from the major disciplines. The
question about Jesus Christ calls for all the resources of
theology and "experimental religion." The questions about
man call upon theology, philosophy, psychology, and sociology
in particular. The questions about becoming call upon theology, psychology, and communications in particular. All are
deeply and normatively influenced by revelation, the gospel,
the word.

A foundation discipline is a field of human investigation
upon whose findings Christian education can build. Certain
"givens" are assumed by the various disciplines. Philosophy
and the sciences assume the givenness of reality. Theology
assumes the givenness of revelation, and that revelation is the
clue to reality.

Man in his attempt to come to terms with reality and revelation, to grasp them and to live with them, has invented or
been given various approaches to them—theological ap-
proaches, social approaches, philosophical approaches, historical approaches, and scientific approaches. These ap-
proaches are symbolized by the disciplinary labels noted above:
theology, philosophy, history, psychology, sociology, and communications.

Theology's scope is the interpretation of revelation and the application of the insights thus derived to the problems of life. Its method is the analysis of its sources, particularly the Scriptures, analysis of experience and religious experience, logical inference, systematics, and consensus. At present there are several schools of theological thought (some associated with particular communions) contending for influence. At the same time there is a healthy beginning of ecumenical theological studies.

The scope of the church's life and work as a discipline is the life, mission, and ministry of the community of faith. Its methods are study, worship, creative expression, action (witness, service, and social action), fellowship (the common life and outreach), stewardship, and all their implications. At present it is highly denominational but with substantial inter-denominational co-operation and the beginnings of an ecumenical consciousness.

Philosophy's scope is the analysis and interpretation of reality (metaphysics), knowledge (epistemology), and value (axiology). Among its active branches are philosophy of history, philosophy of science, philosophy of religion, and philosophy of education. Philosophy of education deals with the educational implications of metaphysics, epistemology, and the theory of value. Its methods center in experience, intuition, and logical analysis. At present there is a proliferation of schools of philosophic thought, with four major "clusters" (naturalism, idealism, realism, and pragmatism) and two "new" interests (existentialism and analytical philosophy).

History's scope as a discipline is the meaningful reconstruction, experiencing, and anticipation of events. Among its branches are history of religion and religious education. The history of education involves the meaningful reconstruction, experiencing, and anticipating of educational events. Its method is selective compilation of data through which various hypotheses may present themselves and be tested. At present, history is highly productive, seeming to be able to provide fruitful hypotheses by which the direction of events may be predicted and controlled.

Psychology's scope is the study of individual personality and behavior. Among its branches are social psychology, psychology of religion, and educational psychology. Educational psychology seeks the educational implications of the study of individual personality and behavior. Psychology's methods are experimental and phenomenological. At present there are several competing schools of thought (behaviorism, Gestalt, Freudian, etc.) with the beginnings of attempts at integration. Psychologists have been active in the investigation and formulation of personality theory, behavior theory, learning theory, motivation theory, and patterns of human growth and development. The counseling and guidance movement has developed within this discipline to a large extent.

The scope of sociology is the study of social groups and movements. Among its branches are urban and rural sociology, sociology of religion, and educational sociology. Educational sociology seeks the educational implications of the study of social groups and movements. Sociology's methods are empirical and logical. At present, it is producing useful hypotheses and insights on social class status, cultural dynamics, and intergroup relations.

The scope of the discipline of communications is the study of the interpenetration of ideas, feelings, and behavior among persons and groups. Its methods are experimental and logical. As a new science, it has not yet become unified in method or outlook but is producing useful hypotheses and insights in such areas as semantics, group dynamics, and symbolics.

The foundation disciplines are, by virtue of their nature and function, continually changing and developing as circumstances alter, as new questions come up, and as new tools of investigation become available. At the present time some significant trends are appearing. The "content" of the disciplines is becoming more highly specialized, detailed, complex, and technical. The boundary lines between the established disciplines are tending to break down, and integrating interdisciplinary investigations are being attempted. While it is impossible at the moment for any one person to comprehend anything like the whole of human knowledge, there is a growing conviction that the important findings in each field must be made available to all in some understandable and usable form.

Education is one of the practical concerns that is helping to bring about the "public" use of much of this material and make it available. In the same way, Christian education is in a position to ask for and use not only all that education gathers from its foundation disciplines but also all that theology and the church can make available.

Indicating the role of the foundation disciplines in education, Herrick and Tyler, in *Toward Improved Curriculum Theory,* describe curriculum theory as consisting of our "working hypotheses" in the educational program (p. iii). Curriculum theory has a threefold task: (1) to identify the critical issues or points in curriculum development and their underlying generalizations; (2) to point up the relationships that exist between these critical points and their supporting structure; (3) to suggest and forecast the future of approaches made to resolve these critical issues (p. 1). The findings of the foundation disciplines may be synthesized into a defensible curriculum theory that will give perspective and direction to efforts to improve educational programs. The disciplines cited are:

> Learning and human development.
> Study of society and its functioning.
> The various areas of human endeavor.
> Instructional practices and educational organization and support. (P. iii.)

In this picture, the ultimate function of curriculum theory is to aid the teacher and his students in the classroom to make more adequate curriculum decisions. (P. 122.) Educational practices based on even poor theory are more open to revision and improvement than practices based on no theory at all. (P. iv.)

The foundation disciplines, then, help us to know what to teach, to know how teaching and learning may be effectively undertaken, and to know how to organize and systematize the teaching-learning process. They provide this help by giving us a clear idea of the field of relationships (God, man, the physical world, and history) with which Christian education deals, and by providing us the raw materials from which we may hammer out the curriculum principles (principles of orientation, design and use and evaluation) that we need.

Christian education curriculum theory is thus constructed by formulating the basic questions that need solving, the questions that need answering; gathering pertinent experience and data from the foundation disciplines; weighing that experience and data; and organizing it in the form of principles.

THEOLOGICAL FOUNDATIONS

Theology's task is to formulate and reformulate Christian beliefs in the light of the word of God and our experience with it, to state the faith of the Christian so that it will be clear to people in the time and community that it is addressing. In other words, it provides the clarifying intellectual thrust of the faith into every culture and every generation. This is a task that is never finished because different cultures and changing ideologies constantly require that the church express its faith in new and appropriate ways.

Protestant theologians in the past have been interested mainly in systematic theology, the logical and thorough development of certain great questions of the Christian religion. Systematic theology has concerned itself with God as sovereign Lord and loving Father; with man as image of God, sinner, and object of redemption; with Jesus Christ as Son of God and Savior; with God's redemptive work on man's behalf; with the Holy Spirit; with the church; with the means of grace; and with the question of destiny. Several American theologians, notably L. Harold DeWolf, Paul Tillich, and Nels F. S. Ferré, have produced creative new approaches to the problems of systematic theology in recent years.

We have just come through a period in which theology was considered to be synonymous with philosophy of religion. The philosophers of religion dwelt on the typical philosophical questions: metaphysics, the question of reality, along with cosmology (What is the universe like?), ontology (the problem of existence), God (his immanence and transcendence), man (Is he good, evil, or neutral?); epistemology, the question of knowledge (Can we know? How? What? How can we be sure?); and axiology, the question of value (What is good? What is beautiful?). Often the philosophers of religion found themselves reviewing systematics and evaluating and reorganizing its findings in terms of some such categories as these.

We now appear to be in a period in which the primary interest is in Biblical theology. Biblical theology's general position is that the Bible, critically understood, is God's revelation on the matters with which theology is concerned. The Bible is the Word of God, and he who attends to it expects to hear God's Word spoken to him. Theology's task is to listen to the Word of God with a trained ear. This means to discover the questions that God himself has raised and to make them the central categories of theological inquiry. It also means to discover what God himself has said and done about these same questions. The receptive and expectant attitude is that for which one prepares by the cultivation of the deepest interpersonal relationships and understanding (substituting, in Buber's terms, for the relationships of "I-it" between persons, in which impersonality prevents real communication, the relationships of "I-Thou," in which true understanding between persons may flourish). Biblical theology tends to reject the interest and concern of systematics for pursuing every problem of Christian thought to its logical conclusion; it rejects the approach of philosophy of religion by starting with revelation rather than with the problems of human thought.

Theology, of course, has a reputation for the complex and the abstruse. As a guide to Christian education some of this difficulty is overcome as theology is asked to answer the questions that persons, in this case Christian educators, are raising. Theology is also being advised by such persons as Martin Buber, Reuel Howe, and Randolph Crump Miller to take account of "the language of relationships," to recognize that the truths and realities with which it deals are not bound up or exhausted in words but rather consist of relationships that may often be experienced and expressed in nonverbal ways. In utter simplicity (as with a primitive culture such as that of the Navaho Indians of a decade or two ago) theology needs the principle of incarnation: instead of trying to say it in abstract terms, the key is to be it, to live it, and to tell the story.

What is the place of theology in the curriculum? Theology has two curricular functions: it is to be taught as subject matter, and it is to be used as a source of insight and direction in determining the context, scope, purpose, process, and design of the curriculum.

As subject matter, theology is to be used by the curriculum maker to assist in teaching about God, man, the physical world, and history in their theological interrelationships and experiential reality. Theology, as subject matter, is learned not only through concepts but also through the experiencing of the relationships to which it refers (as Buber, Howe, and Miller have so convincingly demonstrated). Thus it refers, in both verbal and nonverbal ways, to areas and qualities of experience that are to be encountered and learned.

As a source of insight and direction in determining the context, scope, purpose, process, and design of the curriculum, key educational questions may be put to theology, and thus theological answers to them sought. Just as a hint of what such inquiry might yield, let me suggest the kinds of theological answers that might be given to such questions.

Who teaches? In the final analysis, God is the teacher since he is the living God actively concerned with his people and personally addressing them and since the setting and source of our life is in God and his creative activity. The church, the fellowship of Christ's ministry, is also the teacher. This is where the individual teacher is justified in undertaking his task if he is genuinely of Christ's disciples and called to teach. An interesting question is whether the church tends to lose the deepest meaning of revelation in trying too hard to communicate it.

Who learns? The church learns, as those who are members of the community are nurtured in the faith. The world learns, as the evangelistic thrust of the church reaches it through the teaching ministry.

What is taught and learned? The gospel and the Christian life. The gospel as the story of God's activity and man's response: the Bible. The Christian life in the deepest sense of churchmanship: worship, mission, and faithfulness.

To what purpose? To the end of redemption and fulfillment, that persons may be redeemed in Christ and live in him, that they may receive the gift of eternal life, and that they may join in his mission and ministry.

On what authority? On the authority of the Word of God, testified to by the Holy Spirit in the church.

Where do teaching and learning take place? The loci of teaching and learning are in the person himself, in the church (including the home), and in the community.

When do teaching and learning take place? Fundamentally, in the profound interpersonality of the "I-Thou" encounter, prepared for on the level of person-to-person encounter, and fulfilled at the level of divine-human encounter.

How do teaching and learning take place? Through the use of the means of grace—the ministry of the word, the sacraments, and prayer. Through teaching that consists of inviting to participation in the life and work of the church. Through learning that consists of perceiving the gospel, accepting it, and fulfilling its demands.

How shall teaching and learning experiences be designed and organized? The church as the fellowship of believers in Christ's mission is the clue to design and organization of teaching and learning experiences. Teaching and learning experiences should be designed to *be* the church living its life and doing its work. These experiences will be designed and organized to prepare the learner to respond in faith to God in Christ, to show him how to respond, and to guide him into more mature and effective ways of responding.

BEHAVIORAL FOUNDATIONS

A few psychologists and Christian educators have addressed themselves to the question of the contributions of the behavioral sciences to Christian education theory. Among these were the early psychologists of religion (Starbuck, Coe, James, Pratt, Leuba, and others). Representative of this approach at the present time are Gordon Allport's *The Individual and His Religion,* with chapters entitled "Origins of the Religious Quest," "The Religion of Youth," and "The Religion of Maturity," and Walter H. Clark's *The Psychology of Religion,* which devotes a major section to "Religious Growth."

There are several basic studies of the dynamics of Christian growth by Christian educators. The two most often used are Reuel L. Howe's *Man's Need and God's Action* and Lewis Joseph Sherrill's *The Gift of Power.* Oriented in counseling insights as well as Christian education are Blanche Carrier's *Free to Grow* and Wesner Fallaw's *Toward Spiritual Security.* Strongly theologically oriented, James D. Smart's *The Teaching Ministry of the Church* has a chapter on "The Growth of Persons." Dorothy Arnim and Herman J. Sweet in *Together We Grow* show how growth takes place through relationships and draw conclusions for curriculum and for Christian education administration and leadership.

There are two outstanding studies of religious growth through the life span: Lewis Joseph Sherrill's *The Struggle of the Soul,* and Basil A. Yeaxlee's *Religion and the Growing Mind.*

Much invaluable material on Christian growth has been published in Christian education magazines and quarterlies but has never been gathered and made available for general use. Representative of Christian education books oriented to the growth and guidance of various age levels are Iris V. Cully's *Children in the Church,* Clarice M. Bowman's *Ways Youth Learn,* and Paul V. Maves's *Understanding Ourselves as Adults.*

The lack of definitive material on Christian growth and the somewhat tenuous connection between the materials available on the one hand, and the behavioral studies on the other, suggest that we use as fully as possible the behavioral studies. The most useful will cluster in the fields of personality, motivation, learning, human growth and development, and group and sociocultural understandings.

Calvin S. Hall and Gardner Lindzey, in *Theories of Personality,* provide a thorough and up-to-date review of the major positions on personality. Especially helpful on this matter are the works of Gordon Allport, *Personality: A Psychological Interpretation,* and *Becoming,* and the works of Gardner Murphy, *Personality: A Biosocial Approach,* and *Human Potentialities.*

Being a person means developing those talents and abilities which people have, in contrast to other things and creatures. Each person inherits a temperament, an underlying energy and emotional tone, apparently affected by endocrine glands, nervous system, and other physical and physiological conditions. Each person develops a personality pattern that includes traits, attitudes, interests, values, and ideals largely as a product of interaction with his environment. But the individual's personality may transcend the conditions of his environment, since the developing self is fully as important a determining factor as heredity and environment.

In briefest principle, one might say that interaction between the psychophysical organism and the environmental reality produces the personal individual. For education it is important to remember that the environmental reality is perceived and apprehended in the process and that in this way we gain our concepts of nature, humanity, history, and God.

Personality grows by reaching out for new experience. The term "experience" figures in crucial ways in all educational discussion. Experience is the process of a person's meeting with the world outside and making something of it, and the process of his selecting, organizing, and using in the present what he has made of such encounters with the world outside in the past. The world outside may be persons, things, situations, ideas, symbols, memories, or conditions—past, present, or anticipated. The term "the world outside" is thus not to be taken too literally; perhaps a better way to put it would be "external to the self," if it is remembered that the self of a moment ago may be handled as if it were external to the self. What the person makes of the world outside are feelings, impressions, attitudes, habits, skills, ideas, ideals, and intentions—the key being the process of perception. Several characteristics of experience are noteworthy:

All conscious experience is momentary and contemporary.
Experience is stored up.
Experience is essentially private but may be shared by means of symbols.
The person's experience is a lifelong continuum.
Experience seems to alternate between balance and imbalance throughout life (differentiation and synthesis of experience, reflecting the desire for new experience and the desire for stability).
There seem to be certain kinds of experience that continue throughout life, with variations at different stages, in the manner of variations on a theme.

Ambiguous as the idea of an "outside world" is, there is in experience a definite subjective-objective balance. Experience is essentially personal and private and is hard to share. Yet the most meaningful thing to a human being is to share his experience, which he does through carefully agreed on symbol systems in a context of mutual understanding that takes on the character of fellowship. The symbols used are both verbal and nonverbal. (This is the importance of the symbol of the Word—God getting his experience and purposes across to us so that we share them and doing so in ways we cannot miss.)

Experience provides the raw materials, which personality hammers into shape through the processes of perception and cognition. We invent patterns into which to fit the raw materials of experience as we receive them. When these patterns are inadequate, as they most often are to some degree, we use our intellectual powers, through cognition, to work out the difficulties and inconsistencies, and thus reconstruct our world. "Concepts are the product of a reflective mind busy refining and unifying the numerous elements of experience." Thus we draw the "outside world," which includes much experience of ourselves as well as what is external to us, into our "field of relationships," and create in the process both a personality and a "personal world." The world we perceive, as we perceive and live in it, changes us, and we in turn see ways of changing it, and proceed to act to change it. Part of this is changing ideas; part of it is changing things; part of it is changing circumstances.

Though personality grows through reaching out for new experience, it remains unitary. There is a sense of "I" at the center (which has profound theological implications). There is a sense of personal continuity that embraces past, present, and future. There is a sense of relationships, in which "you," "Thou," and "it" develop in creative tension with "I."

The curriculum is an attempt to help persons to meet certain essentials of the world outside, to guide them in what to make of them, and to help them to select, organize, and use in the present what they have made of such encounters in the past. The curriculum is made up of the best ways yet discovered of coming to grips with life (the major disciplines and subject matter areas—scope) in terms of what is to be experienced, how it is to be experienced, and (once experienced) what it means and how it is to be used.

Motivation is a complex area, since most of the well-known and influential positions (those of Freud, Jung, and Sullivan, for instance) stem from the psychoanalytic schools and have not yet taken on a basic form. The matter is summarized in Gardner Murphy's chapter, "Social Motivation," in Gardner Lindzey's *Handbook of Social Psychology*.

Two aspects of motivation are significant for religion: the motivations that prompt religious experience and the motivations that are engendered by religious experience.

A motive is a psychological linkage between a person (or a group) and an end in view, consisting of a complex of concentrated interest, desire, or dissatisfaction. Motivation involves emotional drive but combines rational and nonrational elements. In a motive, emotion and intellect are concentrated upon a desired object; body and mind become integrated in terms of the achievement of that object. Any given motive will involve the heightening of action along certain lines and the inhibition of other lines of action.

Certain motives are likely to become the sources of personality difficulties, especially if they are out of harmony with, or irreconcilable with, other active motives. This calls for "re-education of the emotions, in terms of carefully and often painfully reconstructed motives." At the same time, no education or growth takes place that is not based on motivation. Motivation is the key to learning.

Hilgard cites Lewin as maintaining that learning is the result of a change of motivation. A desirable outcome may result through a change in the interest and evaluation of the learner. Lewin calls this goal attractiveness, "valence" in the language of chemistry. This may be positive or negative or both positive and negative at the same time. Hilgard, in commenting on Freud, shows the links between motivation, personality, and learning: "If we are to understand the learner as he sets his goals and works realistically toward them, as he is torn by conflicts that prevent his using his abilities, or as he burns himself out in the quest for futile objectives, we need a theory of personality organization incorporated within our general theory of learning" (*Theories of Learning*, p. 324).

Motives may be of different degrees of intensity, from the tentative aim, through the driving urge and the unavowed purpose and desire, to the integrating purpose. Among the most discussed motives in current theory are fear of punishment, hope of reward, pursuit of pleasure, pursuit of wisdom, pursuit of holiness, pursuit of righteousness, altruism, desire for revenge, desire to thwart, need for expression of sex energy, desire for security, desire for social approval, desire for power, need to adjust, and the need to relate to oneself and others. James G. Ranck, in a paper presented at the curriculum study sessions, cites three basic needs: the need to endure, to survive, to "stay alive," to continue to be; the need to "become," to fulfill one's potential; and the need to love and be loved. Behaviorally, he says, these basic needs find expression in:

> The effort to ensure physical survival, involving the nutritive requirements, emotional nurture, and protection from the elements and disease.
> The effort to ensure social physical survival through procreation.
> The effort to become an individual, a self, a person. This involves striving to fulfill one's potential, with concomitant responsibilities of a relative autonomy.
> The effort to become significant, to be valued by one's self and others. This need finds expression in two areas of experience which, while they may be discriminated, are not mutually exclusive: (*a*) in closer, more intimate relationships, where, more subjectively, the need to be loved and to love is operative; (*b*) in wider, less personal relationships, including the "memory

of the race," where, more objectively, the concern is for productivity, achievement and quality and extent of impact.

The need to endure "beyond this present life," which finds expression in the hope of personal immortality. This is more than the hope of survival in the "memory of the race." It is the need to continue to be, in terms of essential, metaphysical selfhood.

All religious experience, because of its involvement with values, is also deeply involved with motivation. But religious experience exhibits a variety of integrating motivations, such as cultivation of the inner life of the spirit, remaking the social order, the conquest of sin, the quest for cosmic security, and the need for self-affirmation.

Some types of religious motivation thwart personality growth (using religious experience to avoid personal autonomy and using religion to repress the vitality of personality). Other types of religious motivation (such as the need for the affirmation of self, one's fellow man, the purpose of life as a whole, and God) aid personality growth.

The various positions on learning are explained and compared in Ernest R. Hilgard's *Theories of Learning*. A useful summary of learning research is found in William Clark Trow's pamphlet *The Learning Process*. The analysis of learning that follows is based substantially upon that developed in my book *The Gospel and Christian Education*.

Education is a teaching-learning process, the key to which is learning. Although in the past the major emphasis has been on the mode of teaching, it is now shifting over to the mode of learning. Learning takes place through perception, practice, problem-solving, and identification. "Perception" is generally intended to suggest the contributions of Gestalt psychology to learning theory; "practice," those of connectionism and reinforcement theory; "problem-solving," those of John Dewey; and "identification," those of depth psychology.

Learning through perception is a blend of insight and discrimination. It is a matter of finding patterns (insight) and signs and cues (discrimination) in the field of experience. The learning takes place when the learner is encouraged to explore a situation (is taken into it systematically) until he sees its inner organization and essential signals and until he sees what it means—grasps or "understands" it. (Murphy calls this the "aha phenomenon.") Then he is encouraged to make it his own through seeing detailed relationships and meanings within it, becoming skilled in responding to it and dealing with it, and using it in the right ways. Once he has the key to the situation, he is at home in it and can, usually rather quickly, make it almost completely his own.

Learning through practice is essentially a matter of training. Traditionally it makes use of the "laws" of readiness, exercise, and effect. "Learning is a process of establishing mental connections, 'bonds,' between stimuli and responses. . . . This is done by massive repetition with appropriate rewards when the learner masters or associates the right response to the right stimulus."

Learning through problem-solving assumes that the person will learn when he is presented with a situation that is somewhat baffling and has to find his way through it. In the process it is thought that he learns to think and that he "learns" the resources that he has to use to solve the problems. The procedure is, as a rule, to define, analyze, suggest possible answers, select the most promising ones, gather the facts, choose the best answer, test it in action, and evaluate it. By this time, several new problems will have popped up that will need solving.

Learning through identification involves "the appropriation into the self of the characteristics of an admired group or person" (*Dictionary of Education*). The learner associates and classifies himself with the admired group or person, and through analysis, imitation, worship, and the like, incorporates into his personality the desired qualities. Recent studies have shown that values are effectively "interiorized and internalized" through identification.

Our task in Christian education, since a coherent and inclusive theory of learning is lacking, would seem to be to try to be clear about what we want to teach (analyzing it in such terms as facts, ideas, skills, habits, attitudes, appreciations, and values), and to sort out these learnings in terms of what may best be learned through perception, through practice, through problem-solving, or through identification, and to pick our methods and procedures accordingly. A beginning at this might yield such an analysis as the following:

Facts, such as the events of the life of Jesus or the history of the church, might be learned either through perception or through practice, depending upon their context and use. Such methods as reading, study, discussion, analysis, memorization, and drill might be appropriate.

Ideas, such as the Trinity or human destiny, might be learned best through perception, in which case methods like reading, study, and discussion could be used.

Skills, such as prayer and worship, would require a good deal of practice, calling for analysis, memorization, and drill.

Other skills, such as social action, would call for considerable problem-solving in addition to practice and would therefore involve the use of projects.

Habits (closely related to skills), such as Bible study, might call for practice if they were narrowly conceived or might call for all types of learning if they were broadly conceived. (This illustrates the difficulties involved in habit theories of learning.)

Attitudes, such as loyalty and love, might call for problem-solving and identification, thus using methods such as discussion, projects, meditation, other devotional acts, and music and the arts.

Appreciations, such as understanding the word of God and the meaning of the sacraments, would call for all four types of learning but would certainly not be complete without identification.

Values, such as stewardship or discipleship, would seem to involve all four again but primarily perception, problem-solving, and identification. The chief Christian value, the life in Christ, is the most integral, demanding, and meaningful identification possible; it inextricably involves also identification with the church, his body.

The analysis of the aspects of Christian learning is obviously extremely fluid and must remain so to be effective. Only so may the dangers of artificiality in such an analysis be avoided. Not only must the "aspects" be considered as fluid but also the application of types of learning to those aspects and the development of methodological implications. Despite its possible artificiality, however, this provides Christian education with one of its most important areas of research.

Currently, a great deal of learning theory is being reduced to and used in connection with the idea of developmental tasks, or with the idea of learning tasks. This approach articulates well with the analytical approach above but avoids its artificiality and has the advantage of looking at learning from the learner's point of view, following the process along as it takes place. The "learning-tasks" approach views learning as a process of human becoming through experience in a field of relationships which is comprehensive.

The learning-tasks idea is built on the hypothesis that human becoming, including Christian becoming, involves the development of personality, which may be defined in terms of the categories of meaning and value. Further, true becoming involves conversion in the light of the gospel. (The time factor provides a difficulty for Christian education at this point, some affirming infant regeneration within the context of the covenant and thus having to deal with questions of infant baptism, the improvement of baptism, and confirmation, others affirming the regeneration of believers alone—and thus confronting questions of the status of children in the church.)

The learning-tasks idea is also built on the hypothesis that the experience of becoming involves a chronology in which five processes of human becoming occur and recur: exploration (getting to know), discovery of meaning and value (understanding and appreciating), personal appropriation of meaning and value (making it one's own), conversion of meaning and value (confessing and accepting the gospel), and assumption of responsibility (doing things about it). There is an inherent progression in the first three, even though the cycle is often broken and often repeated. Conversion of meaning and value is the essential condition for education that is distinctively Christian. Assumption of responsibility is the essential condition for the maintenance of existence. In a sense then in Christian education the last two processes are constantly operative, while the first three "spiral" around them.

Representative of horizontal studies in human growth and development is Elizabeth B. Hurlock's *Developmental Psychology*. The outstanding longitudinal studies are John P. Zubek and P. A. Solberg's *Human Development* and Sidney L. Pressey and Raymond G. Kuhlen's *Psychological Development Through the Life Span*. Erik H. Erikson's *Childhood and Society* is oriented to psychoanalysis and anthropology. Robert J. Havighurst's *Human Development and Education* is an attempt to put the findings of the behavioral sciences on human development in a form that will be usable in education, as is Arthur T. Jersild's *Child Development and the Curriculum*. There are also many studies on child and adolescent psychology but a strange dearth of materials on adult psychology.

There is a dramatic movement of personality through life, involving ages and stages: infancy, childhood, youth, maturity, old age. Each has its distinctive features, defined by certain needs and characteristic modes of fulfilling those needs. Yet the ages and stages merge into one another rather imperceptibly.

The reality of individual consciousness takes precedence over the idea of ages and stages, however, in determining what we do in Christian education. That is why curriculums too closely geared to standardized age-level understandings have to be adapted so often and so radically, and why we have to change carefully laid plans. What we generalize about ages and stages must be co-ordinated with the developing self (in its favor) at every point.

Erikson, in *Childhood and Society,* has provided an interesting analysis of the achievements that lead to maturity, to which the tasks contribute: the sense of trust, the sense of autonomy, the sense of initiative, the sense of industry, the sense of identity, the sense of intimacy, the sense of generativity, and the sense of integrity. Placing these as he does in terms of a dialectic tension between adequacy and inadequacy at each level, Erikson has succeeded in bringing depth psychology into focus for the educator.

James G. Ranck, in his paper for the curriculum study committee, shows how a "developmental shifting" takes place in the dominance of various basic needs in the different age periods:

> In infancy and childhood, the need for physical survival and security, and for "unconditional acceptance," appears to be dominant.
>
> In preadolescence and adolescence, the dominant needs are (a) to "belong," and (b) to be free. This is often an exceptionally traumatic period, involving the dilemmas of (a) sacrificing autonomy for the acceptance of peers, and (b) sacrificing acceptance of authority figures for freedom. Typically, this "freedom" is initially spurious, since the basically healthy need to be free is acted out in self-defeating negativism, rebellion, and defiance.
>
> In the young adult, the dominant need is for social physical survival, which finds expression in the sex drive, procreation, and in being loved and learning to love in a family context which is heavily charged with needs for physical expressions of affection.
>
> In the "mature" adult the dominant need is for personal and social significance. Qualitatively, the individual is concerned to be valued highly, both by himself and others, and quantita-

tively, he desires to register maximum impact on the "memory of the race."

In old age, the need for security is again dominant, but it now finds expression primarily in a concern to be reassured of acceptance and significance.

Gradually, in a way that combines exploration, experimentation, and the reorganization and refinement of experience, the child gets to know his world and comes to grips with it. Naturally, many of the child's perceptions are fragmentary and tentative. They need enlarging, enriching, remaking, and refining. It is the process of education that helps to expedite this. Education becomes a little more understandable and manageable when the educator realizes how engrossed the child is in perceiving, and when he sees his task as helping out in the process. Infancy is a period of complete dependence, with a reaching out, and the beginnings of control. Early childhood is a period of gaining control of oneself and one's environment, primarily through the increased use of the tools of communication. Late childhood is a period of mastery of the tools of communication, learning to live in an expanding world, and getting ready for release from dependence. In Christian education the chief task of childhood is perceiving the gospel. This means exploring the gospel (seeing, hearing, getting acquainted), experimenting with the gospel (activities and projects in which one's ideas and insights are tried out), and organizing and refining one's thoughts and feelings on the gospel (thought, prayer, talk). Several important things must be kept in mind. The child is "on the way"; he has not arrived; this is, in effect, the major factor involved. There are many elements involved in the gospel for the child—the whole expanding field of relationships, with special attention to the Bible, the faith, prayer and worship, hymns, Christian art, festivals, the home, the church, Jesus Christ, etc. When he perceives the gospel, he is no longer, strictly speaking, a child—for in perhaps a rudimentary way he sees clearly the meaning of history and the meaning of existence.

Adolescence involves self-realization—the achievement of a sense of personal identity. For Christian education, self-realization is basically a matter of accepting the gospel, in the fullest sense: coming to self-realization by learning to respond in the Spirit of God to the love offered him in the gospel (this is the heart of the matter of accepting the gospel), and coming to self-realization by using the perspective of his point of view and his system of values in dealing as a Christian with the problems that confront him (this is accepting the implications of the gospel).

Young adulthood is often a period of rapid increase in responsibilities and effective living. Middle adulthood is often a period of steady accomplishment and effective leadership. Old age may lessen responsibilities and offer a more relaxed enjoyment of life's good. The chief adult task in Christian education is the progressive discovery of the implications of the gospel and the fulfilling of these implications. Thus the adult will remain receptive to new experience, achieve mature discrimination in values, achieve integrity of religious experience, speak the language of religion with meaning and conviction, and achieve social effectiveness in vocation and in other types of Christian action.

There are exceptional persons whose growth does not follow the process as it has been outlined. Furthermore, we cannot expect that every person at each age level, even when given the opportunity, will carry out the tasks especially suited to his development. The person endeavoring to communicate the faith, as well as the learner himself, needs to be helped to bear this in mind and not to feel defeated or discouraged.

What is known of the influence of groups on personality and growth is summarized in Dorwin Cartwright and Alvin Zander's *Group Dynamics, Research and Theory*. Group dynamics and sociocultural insights are related to education in Howard Lane and Mary Beauchamp's *Human Relations in Teaching*.

The culture provides the basic norms and values that surround the individual and, through interaction, help to make him what he is to become. The culture expresses itself in many ways: customs, the rituals and symbols of the community, folklore, literature, doctrine, religion, and the like. The culture influences but does not absolutely determine what the individual will become. His response to the culture may be selective, in which case individuality is preserved and enhanced. In this case the culture sustains but does not imprison the individual.

The culture is communicated through the community, the family, and other groups. In education, the small group has been found to be especially effective both in the socialization and the individualization of personality. Through training the person to participate in the group process, analyze tasks and movements within the group, discover and evaluate roles, find and weigh such factors as "hidden agenda," gain skill in helping the group of which he is a member to decide on goals and structure itself, learn to evaluate results objectively, and the like, group experience enables him to achieve the delicate balance of independence and participation that in many ways is the key to contemporary living.

Personality development involves the three interrelated dynamic processes of maturation (this is the individual in relation to himself), acculturation (this is the individual in relation to his community), and emotional security (this is the quality of life that he makes out of both these relationships). With all three—growth in community in its proper place—development of a balanced sort may take place.

Guidance for curriculum. Certain insights emerge from the consideration of the contributions of the behavioral sciences which, when seen in a theological light, provide basic guidance for the orientation of the curriculum:

Human becoming is the continuous, lifelong process of sharing those meanings and values that define who we are.

Human becoming takes place in common human relationships.

There is an urge to communicate our discoveries, our needs, our frustrations, ourselves as we are in process of becoming.

We communicate the way we perceive, and in the very process of communicating, we perceive afresh.

Communication is a transaction, the partners to which are:

The living God: Father, Son, and Holy Spirit (Creator, Redeemer, critical and revitalizing Presence). The living God communicates himself in the Word (the Word to his people, the Word made flesh, the record of the Word, the word spoken to me, the word spoken to us, the word spoken through us).

The church: the nurturing and directing community of worship, witness, and work.

The teacher: a person in process of becoming, with an urge to communicate.

The learner: a person in process of becoming, with an urge to communicate.

The community: the local social body through which the culture (and conflicts in cultures) is communicated.

The culture: the values, ways, and standards that identify a people. (Language, customs, doctrine, folklore, religion.)

The family: the most intimate social body, held together by the bond of love, communicating life's basic values and ways.

The communicative transaction requires contact, mutuality (give-and-take), sensitivity and understanding, integrity, response and investment (response implies investment if hypocrisy is not to ensue), and accuracy of translation.

A curriculum, as was said at the beginning of the book, is a comprehensive plan by which the teaching-learning process may be systematically undertaken. Devise a plan for the communicative transaction, involving the various partners to the transaction but centering upon a learner or a learning group, and you have a curriculum.

THE EXAMINATION OF PRINCIPLES

Protestant curriculum has for many years placed great emphasis upon three principles: comprehensiveness, balance, and sequence. The principle of comprehensiveness has held that the curriculum must be inclusive of every curriculum element (every aspect of life, experience, and subject matter that is of concern in the Christian life). This principle is now being reinterpreted in terms of the principle of scope.

The principle of balance has held that every curriculum element must be given its proper weight at each point in the curriculum. The function of this principle is now seen as being performed by the organizing principle.

The principle of sequence has held that there must be an apparent progression in content and experience; related areas of curriculum should be arranged to provide for cumulative learnings and through them incentives to appropriate commitment and action. This principle, still considered valid, is one of the key principles in design of the curriculum.

In late years, a fourth principle has been discussed and used, the principle of flexibility. The principle of flexibility holds that the curriculum should be changeable and adaptable in terms of the educational settings where it is to be used, in terms of method, and in terms of individual, community, and cultural differences. Also valid, this principle, like that of sequence, is one of the key principles in design of the curriculum.

The present proposal, growing out of the considerations of the book so far, is that we need at least the following curriculum principles:

A principle of context.

A principle of scope.

A principle of purpose.

A principle of process.

An organizing principle and a means for implementing it. Two principles of design: sequence and flexibility.

In terms of theology and the behavioral sciences, these principles will have to be sound and adequate. Perhaps the key tests that ought to be applied are these: Are they framed clearly in the light of the gospel? Do they take into account adequately the learner's native equipment, his world (his environment and its influences on him), how he grows, what he seeks (motivation), and how he learns?

Chapter 5

FUNDAMENTAL CURRICULUM PRINCIPLES

I F THE CURRICULUM is a plan by which the teaching-learning process may be systematically undertaken by the church, the fundamental principles toward which it must be oriented are principles of context, scope, purpose, and process. Such principles will provide basic guidance concerning where Christian education and its curriculum take place, what content is involved, the underlying purpose that guides them, and the orientation for method. Moving from these first principles to the question of curriculum itself, we will explore an organizing principle and the means of satisfactorily implementing it.

CONTEXT

The question of the context of Christian education and its curriculum is the question of their normative surroundings. Where, basically, does Christian education take place? Among the answers that have been seriously suggested are that Christian education takes place where the Bible is taught, where instruction in Christian doctrine takes place, where the Christian life is lived and shared, where the good society exists and educates, or where the church lives its life and does its work.

On an even more practical level, the locale of Christian education is the church school class, the church club, the home, the play group, the youth group, the vacation church school, or the weekday church school. But these are just the places that we have invented to represent *the* place where the teaching-learning transaction takes place. They are nothing in themselves if the essential conditions are not present, and the essential conditions define *the* place.

For Christian education to take place, there must be a learner, a person, a growing, developing, relating individual. The transaction takes place here, or it does not take place at all. But the individual in isolation is utterly without meaning.

For Christian education to take place, then, the "surroundings" are also of real importance. The culture largely determines and mediates attitudes, values, language, and emotional moorings. Significant roles are played by the public school, by the community, by the play group, and by the larger world in all its wonder, variety, immensity, challenge, opportunity, beauty, horror, and terror. Christian education without the church (local, denominational, and ecumenical) in the "surroundings" is unthinkable There are also the "planned" surroundings of Christian education: the church school, the home, and the community agencies. For education to take place, the teaching-learning process provides the way in which meaning may be established through association with such surroundings in the process of becoming, the key being a communicative transaction with the surroundings.

Fundamentally, Christian education takes place where the community of persons in Christ worships, witnesses, and works. This community has a life, a message, a mission, and a heritage; brought into being, sustained, and directed by God, it continues his reconciling work in Jesus Christ. The gospel is its message; the Holy Spirit is its power; love is its mood. The life it lives and the work it does are as varied as the expressions it finds in the home, the school, the neighborhood, the congregational life and worship, the missionary enterprise, Christian service and social action, and all the ways in which the ecumenical spirit is brought to reality. Christian education in this context is nurture in the fellowship of love.

This community of worship, witness, and work is up against the world. The gospel is for the world; the church exists to bear the message of God's reconciling and redeeming love to those who need to hear and accept it. The Holy Spirit makes this witness possible, and at the same time feeds and guides the worshiping community. The fellowship of love and of work is an open-ended fellowship, always ready to receive those who have responded to the good news or who want to hear it.

At the same time, the community of worship, witness, and work is up against itself. It is both God's people and also a human community. This means the need for constant renewal of its own life, a renewal that is accomplished not so much by seeking it directly, as by losing its life in worship and service (by directing itself toward God and its fellow men), and like its Lord "taking the form of a servant."

There is thus no hard and fast line that separates the church from the world. When in Christian education we speak of education in the church, we do not mean to set up a category of those "on the outside," excluded. If some exclude themselves, the church is still their servant; if some have never been reached, the church has the imperative of mission to them.

Part of its "innerness" is that the church remembers and reflects. Much of its worship, liturgical and nonliturgical, consists of acts of remembrance and reflection. The sermon is the first example of this, if it is a sermon in which the preacher tries to enable the congregation to hear the word of God. The sacraments and the festivals are times of remembrance and reflection within the fellowship. Then in the midst of its remembrance and reflection the church acts in mission and ministry.

The worshiping, witnessing, working community of persons in Christ may be said to be the definitive locale of Christian education and its curriculum, since without the dynamic reality of the community of faith, Christian meaning cannot be communicated.

Practical questions arise, however, about this principle. Is this community the local congregation, or is it the denomination, or is it the church around the world and eternal? As one of the participants in the joint curriculum study put it: "Must I be specifically trying to root the young people whom I'm teaching on Sunday morning in a Christian community that quite transcends the local congregation and denomination, or may I be content with their rootage in the formal fellowship of their own church? I should hope that a larger community was intended and might well be made explicit in the curriculum."

The curriculum builder, trying for instance to guide the study of the Bible, finds himself frustrated in his purpose if he cannot depend on the church in which the study is to take place reflecting its own true nature. The ethos in which the teaching takes place may be something entirely different. The pupil gradually learns to understand and use in thinking and communication the language of those with whom he lives. If the record of revelation is taken lightly by the church, represented by the teacher and the class, no matter how good the teaching is the Bible will be taken lightly by the pupil. The effectiveness of teaching methods will be undercut by the ethos because they are in contradiction. Such a church is not a worshiping, witnessing, working community and therefore is not the context for Christian education. What is needed in such a situation is a major emphasis on adult education and leadership education, alongside the curriculum, to make the local congregation conscious of ways in which it may become the community of faith.

The communication of the faith, then, requires an active, believing community that is reaching out from itself as an instrument of God's evangelization of the world. Education in the Christian faith cannot be carried on outside this context. But where do you find such a community? The fact is that, while we find in the church a great deal that denies the nature of the community of faith, there is a vital core of community in those who are constantly being "renewed" within the church, those who have a genuine and compelling commitment to Christ. Where there is even such a core there is a community that will transmit its faith. When something of the body of Christ may be sensed in the little microcosm of the Christian community in the local church and even in the class, there is something of a favorable learning situation for Christian education.

The same participant in the study cited above, spoke to this point: "I suspect that in the earlier years the child is not going to be influenced very much by the larger body of Christ. He will to some extent if the teacher in the class and other people in the church are themselves very much a part of the larger Christian community. Some of the overtones and suggestions of that larger membership will even filter through to the smaller child. But by the time he comes to high school age, he becomes very much concerned with knowing the extent of the community of which he is a part. By that time we need to be especially clear whether we are going to try to keep him in bounds, to keep his loyalty attached to this particular branch of Christendom, or whether we are going to seek quite explicitly to make him feel that he is a part of the whole body of Christ, which reaches around the world and across many denominational barriers."

In a community there are two languages, the language of relationships and the spoken language. The spoken language of the community and its unspoken relationships are in the long run inseparable, at least in the sense that they must be in harmony with each other. We are increasingly aware of the nonverbal elements in Christian communication: the atmosphere of the Christian home and the life of a community of Christians with a spirit of love, trust, and integrity. Yet the nonverbal must in time be verbalized if it is to be understood. This raises specifically the problem of language, vocabulary, and its role in Christian education. The key to this question is that the appropriate language is the language that the community uses in a vital way to express the heart of its faith and life.

What is language for? Words have three functions: to point out (helping us to gain experience), to formulate (helping us to organize experience), and to communicate (helping us to share experience). Vocabulary is invented in the process of gaining, organizing, and sharing new meanings. Sometimes, with effort, it is redeemed.

Vocabulary creates and reflects our patterns of thought and life. Some people think concretely, some abstractly, and their vocabularies reflect this fact. There are different ways in different cultures for stating the nature of truth and for apprehending truth. Again, their words reflect this. The English language has its peculiar problems because it is a conglomeration of Greek, Latin, Anglo-Saxon, and other patterns of thought and life.

Christian education deals with the vocabulary of the gospel and the Word of God. The Word of God is his way of revealing himself to us. It has been a spoken word; it is the Word made flesh in Jesus Christ; it is the written word, the Bible, witnessed to by the Holy Spirit. God's own language is quite clearly a combination of the spoken and the unspoken, the verbal and the nonverbal, a language of words and a language of relationships: he acts, he talks, he shows, he sends, he waits; he enters, he heals, he teaches, he preaches, he prays; he suffers, he dies, he rises, he ascends, he lives and reigns; he returns; and through it all he creates, he loves, and he redeems.

Our challenge is to be able to speak in lives and at the same time in words that learners can understand accurately, that can get through to them, making things clear to them, and helping them in turn to be able to speak a language that expresses their faith and life.

With this emphasis upon the social context for Christian education, the counterbalancing fact must be kept in mind that many people have come to a living experience of God in spite of the social environment in which they live. The Holy Spirit is not "contained" in the church; the Holy Spirit is given to the church in order that it may have life and be the church as a fellowship with a mission and ministry. The church witnesses to the Holy Spirit; it does not mediate the Holy Spirit. But the kind of community in which we forbear one another in love and build up the unity of the Spirit in the bond of peace should not be downgraded in our minds. To the extent that the church is at the disposal of the Holy Spirit, it will tend to foster a living experience of God over against the social environment and even over against itself. The Biblical perspective is that God's relations are primarily with a people whom he loves, corrects, and redeems, and also with individuals who are part of that people or who have to do with that people.

Education in the worshiping, witnessing, working community of persons in Christ means that such a community must exist in some form or other, and that teacher and learner must participate in its worship, witness, and work. The nurture, the instruction, the action, and the review and renewal that are implied constitute the learning process in Christian education. The principle may be developed in order to show its essential ingredients, relationships, and implications:

The church is true to its basic nature when it is the worshiping, witnessing, and working community of persons in Christ.

The source of the community's witness is the Word of God, revelation, and the gospel.

Christian education (along with other functions) is one of the essential ministries of the worshiping, witnessing, working community.

It is the worshiping, witnessing, working community that does Christian education. The congregation does Christian education in so far as it is that community. The family does Christian education in so far as it is that community.

Christian education should especially concentrate on the task of adult education. The Christian education of children and youth should be primarily the task of the home in the case of Christian families and closely linked with the evangelistic task in the case of those not from Christian families.

The educational work of the Christian congregation should observe the following priorities: (1) First priority should be given to those educational needs and activities that may be carried on by the congregation as a whole or by ungraded groups within the congregation. (2) Second priority should be given to those educational needs and activities that can be carried on by families. (3) Third priority should be given to those educational needs and activities that can best be done in graded groups, but in this case every effort must be maintained to see that there is congregational co-ordination of the work of these groups.

The institutional forms of Christian education should be subjected to constant restudy and change, in order that the work of the Christian community may be effectively related to the needs of its time and setting and not hampered by the inertia of loyalty to accepted but obsolete forms.

SCOPE

The use of the term "scope" arises out of considerations of trying to differentiate among various types of objectives. It refers generally to the substance or content of curriculum. In an effort at precision, "scope of Christian education" is used for this purpose, while "purpose of Christian education" is used to denote the basic objective. The term "scope" is an obvious one to substitute for that of "comprehensiveness" in referring to curriculum substance or content.

When scope is discussed it must be borne in mind that many different terms have been used in the past to designate what is meant. Some of the more common references to scope are in terms of essential curriculum content, areas of curricular experience, areas of subject matter, curriculum elements, themes, general objectives, the great concerns of the Christian faith and the Christian life, and centers of attention within the field of relationships. We may assume that these are all attempts to get at the same thing, that with which Christian education deals, the scope of the curriculum. The basic problem of scope is that of being comprehensive (omitting no important element or experience) and at the same time producing a picture that is unified, manageable, and reduced to the absolute minimum.

The magnitude of the problem is evident when we remember the aspects and experiences of life that will be comprehended in the curriculum: God, his revelation, his work, and his church; the physical world; society and culture; the learner's growth and development; his coming to grips with the Christian faith; his growth in the Christian life; and his membership and work in the church.

The approaches to scope in various recent curriculum documents are as follows:

Junior High Objectives: God, Jesus Christ, man, the social order, the church, and the Bible.

The Objectives of Christian Education: Christian self-realization and personal maturity, social relationships, the natural world and the conservation of its values, the Bible and the Christian heritage, and responsible churchmanship.

The Objective of Christian Education for Senior High Young People: Personality (the world of persons and the self), the family, the community, the world (the larger society), the natural world, history, and the church and the gospel.

United Presbyterian: The Lord of Christian faith and life, the Bible in Christian faith and life, and the church in Christian faith and life.

Protestant Episcopal: The Holy Scriptures, church history, the faith of the church, the worship of the church, Christian living, and the Episcopal Church and its work.

Methodist: God, man, Jesus Christ, the Bible, the church, history, and Christian living.

Lutheran: God, the Christian church, the Bible, the pupil's fellow men, the physical world, and the pupil himself.

Presbyterian U.S.: The Bible as witness and instrument, the church as witness and instrument, the nature and need of man, and the character of the new life in Christ.

United Church of Christ: God, man, Jesus Christ, the Holy Spirit.

United Church of Canada: God and his purpose, Jesus Christ and the Christian life, and the church and the world.

Several other statements should be taken into account at this point:

Objectives of Christian Education (from *Christian Education Today,* 1940): God, Jesus Christ, Christlike character, Christian social order, churchmanship, Christian family, Christian philosophy of life, Bible, and other materials.

Youth Program Areas (1951): Christian faith, Christian witness, Christian outreach, Christian citizenship, and Christian fellowship.

A Guide for Curriculum in Christian Education (1955): Forty-two areas are listed, grouped under headings: the Bible, faith or beliefs, personal experiences in Christian living, Christian family, church life and outreach, social problems, world relations, and service and Christian leadership.

The Study of Christian Education (1946–1947): The changing needs and experiences of the individual; God, as revealed in Jesus Christ; the individual's fellow men and human society; his place in the work of the world; the Christian fellowship, the church; the continuous process of history, viewed as a carrier of the divine purpose and revealer of the moral law; and the universe in all its wonder and complexity.

Certain areas of agreement are clear when comparison is

made of such statements as these. The issues are perhaps not so clear. One of the issues is that of the theological orientation of statements and analyses of scope. Is the scope of Christian education the scope of education plus some Christian elements, or is the scope of Christian education the whole field of relationships in the light of the gospel? Another issue is that of representative elements. May Christian education do its job adequately by selecting certain key elements (like the Bible, Christian ethics, etc.), and by limiting its scope to these elements? Or, again, must it be concerned with all relationships in the light of the gospel? There is a difference between the selection of representative elements, about which real questions may be raised, and the reduction of all elements to their essentials. The one is selective, the other comprehensive.

In the course of the joint curriculum study a summary statement of scope was presented that served as a basis for discussion and work. Later, the statement was reordered. The original statement is presented here, however, to show the elements with which the study worked:

> The curriculum is involved with the interaction of the person with his whole field of relationships in the light of the gospel.
>
> The personal individual is the product of the interaction of a psychophysical organism and its environmental reality. The environmental reality is perceived and apprehended in the process. That environmental reality may be described in terms of the dimensions of nature, humanity, history, and the divine. It may be dealt with by the Christian in terms of the following centers of attention:
>
> *God*—Father, Son, and Holy Spirit, making himself known through the Word, working in and through the church.
>
> *Man*—as he was created (in the image of God), as he is (sinner), and as he may become (redeemed), as self, in common human relationships, culture and heritage.
>
> *The physical world*—as the setting in which God has created man to live.
>
> *History*—as the continuum of God's activity and man's life.

One of the major accomplishments of the study was its careful revision of the suggested formulation of the scope of Christian education and its curriculum. Before presenting the revision, the reasoning of the study should be explored briefly.

The very fact that God is a living reality, coming to man in Jesus Christ, and confronting persons at every point in their existence, makes it possible for us to avoid "including God in the scope of Christian education," as if he were something to be learned about, like some of the other elements in the field of relationships. The scope of Christian education must explicity provide for the fact of God's relatedness to man in a dynamic way.

This means that the elements in the field of relationships must be described in detail in the light of the gospel, especially as to their qualities of relatedness, and not merely listed, which might give the impression of their being dealt with in an equal and homogeneous way. Furthermore, the elements in the field of relationships in the light of the gospel will have to be explicitly weighed in any statement of the scope of Christian education. Taking these matters into account, the reformulation of the statement of the scope of Christian education and its curriculum was made as follows:

God (Father, Son, and Holy Spirit) comes to man in the Word, made known to us in the Bible and in the life of the church, calling us into relationship with him and thus throwing the light we need on:

Man—so that we see and relate to him as he was created (in the image of God), as he is (sinner), and as he may become (redeemed):

as self,

in common human relations,

as the creator, possessor, and transmitter of the culture and heritage;

Nature—so that we see and relate to it as the setting in which God has created man to live;

History—so that we see and relate to it as the continuum of God's activity and man's life.

The rationale for such a statement lies in the concept of "the field of relationships" and "the field of relationships in the light of the gospel," which was explored in *The Objective of Christian Education for Senior High Young People* (pp. 21–22). The four paragraphs that follow are a review of, and commentary on, that rationale.

The person's world is the field of his relationships. It is in terms of this field of relationships that Christian education takes place. The field of relationships provides the setting for Christian education, constituting as it does the scene of the person's relationships or the field of his experience. It could mean his environment if that term were given a sufficiently broad construction.

The person cannot see the field of relationships whole, but he can group it in terms of its dimensions: the divine, the human, nature, and history. Put another way, the setting of Christian education is perceived in terms of God, man, the natural world, all with past, present, and future reference. What are called the dimensions of the setting of Christian education are ways of describing the nature and extent of that setting. Our perception of our world, but not in the light of the gospel, might lead us to see the dimensions of experience as God (creator, ruler, cause, ultimate source of being, and goal of existence), man (a biosocial organism, endowed with personality, selfhood, and a moral nature), nature (a universe of cause and effect, natural law, and contingency), and history (cycles or lines of existence, sometimes seen as meaningful, sometimes not).

In Christian education, all four dimensions must be taken into account. However, the normative dimension of Christian education is the divine revelation. This is true because through revelation God has provided man with the necessary perspective from which to see the essential meaning and significance of the other dimensions. Our perception of our world in the light of the gospel means that we hear the word of God, witnessed to in the Bible and the church, spoken about in the dimensions of existence. Nature, man, and history remain in essence obscure, purposeless, and evil until they are seen and accepted in the light of God's self-disclosure in his Word and his redemptive action on man's behalf in the gospel of his seeking love in Jesus Christ. In this sense the scope of the curriculum is the word of God.

As persons are aware of God's self-disclosure and seeking love in Jesus Christ and respond in faith and love, they come to know who they really are—sons of God (as redeemed sinners who in Christ may fulfill the meaning of personality)—and what their human situation (past, present, and future) means; grow as sons of God rooted in the Christian community (the church); live in the Spirit of God in every relationship (the heart of the matter in ethics and social responsibility); fulfill their common discipleship—implying stewardship—in the world (the family, the community, and the larger society); and abide in the Christian hope. All this is done responsibly against the background of the dimension of nature.

Because the factor of human perception and the growth of experience is involved, there is an element of continuity to be taken into account in Christian education. The curriculum is to be planned to facilitate a continuing communicative trans-action between the person and the field of his relationships in the light of the gospel.

Further light may be cast on the problem of the scope of Christian education by showing how scope is "seen" at various levels of apprehension and for various purposes: as the dimensions of experience (the categories of perception), as the field of relationships, as the field of relationships in the light of the gospel, as the scope of Christian education itself, as themes, as topics, as problems, and as group and individual goals:

In determining the scope of Christian education, the place to begin is with the fundamental *dimensions of experience,* which are the *categories of perception* (the divine, the human, the natural, and the historical).

Since these represent the real as perceived, since they are dimensions of experience, a focus in the person or persons perceiving is implied. They therefore become *the field of persons' relationships.*

The Christian theologian or philosopher of religion, approaching the matter analytically, sees *the field of relationships in the light of the gospel,* since the gospel tells us who God is, who man is, what nature is, and what history is. From this vantage point the scope of Christian education would be as originally stated.

Christian education, however, must weigh the field of relationships in the light of the gospel as experienced, since in Christian education we deal with God, man, nature, and history as Biblically and existentially perceived. *The scope of Christian education*—comprehensive, inclusive, and weighed Biblically and existentially, becomes that of the revised formulation.

From this basic idea of the scope of Christian education, there are a number of justifiable ways in which curriculum *themes* may be formulated, stated, and used.

There are likewise a number of ways in which *topics* (specific elements related to the themes to be used for the building of units) may be derived from the themes.

In the same way, there are a number of varied ways in which *problems* (topics encountered) may be used in curriculum.

This idea of scope, allowing for a variety of approaches to themes, topics, and problems, allows also for a great variety of *group and individual goals* (ways of dealing with the problems) in the classroom, in individual work, and in informal groups.

Parenthetically, the progression of this analysis emphasizes again that group and individual goals (learning tasks in very specific form) are the point at which the two great streams, the person and the faith, meet in Christian education curriculum. Learning tasks and group and individual goals are required to carry the whole burden of motivations and objectives on the one hand and the scope of Christian education on the other.

In terms of such a concept of the scope of Christian education, as has been proposed, the Bible has an evident and central function. "The task of Biblical theology," as Holmes Rolston puts it, "is to make us hear what the original writers meant to say to their original readers, and to face its relevance for us. No curriculum can avoid a place for just that kind of Bible study." Carrying out the learning tasks in the light of the gospel requires that priority be given to the task of "listening with growing alertness to the gospel." Such a task is impossible without serious, thorough, and continuous Bible study at the heart of the process. The whole field of relationships must be seen in light of the gospel, in Biblical perspective.

PURPOSE

What is the purpose of the curriculum? The purpose of the curriculum is the purpose of Christian education—that the whole field of relationships may be seen and dealt with in this new perspective of the gospel, this Biblical perspective:

> The objective of Christian education is to help persons to be aware of God's self-disclosure and seeking love in Jesus Christ and to respond in faith and love—to the end that they may know who they are and what their human situation means, grow as sons of God rooted in the Christian community, live in the Spirit of God in every relationship, fulfill their common discipleship in the world, and abide in the Christian hope. (From *The Objective of Christian Education for Senior High Young People*.)

The heart of the objective is in awareness and response—awareness of revelation and the gospel (God's self-disclosure and seeking love in Jesus Christ), and response in faith and love. The rest of the statement (what follows "—to the end that . . .") indicates the major contextual areas of experience involved in Christian faith and life, and the difference that serious attention to the objective of awareness and response to revelation and the gospel will make in each of them. The clear distinction between the objective of the church and the objective of Christian education lies at exactly this point. Christian education's task is to invite individuals to such awareness and response as will help to achieve the objective of the church. The church's objective is, of course, inclusive of that of Christian education, but if Christian education has a distinctive role it is at this point of invitation to awareness and response.

Because the objective uses the phrases, "God's self-disclosure and seeking love in Jesus Christ," there has been an occasional sense of confusion that was voiced by one participant in the study in this way: "This statement just as it stands is likely to seem limited to the revelation through Jesus Christ. Do we mean to align ourselves with what many are calling a Christo-cratic view, which is being accused of being a unitarianism of the second person of the Trinity? Do we believe no longer that God reveals himself in the creation? Do we believe no longer that God reveals himself as Holy Spirit directly to our hearts?"

Speaking for myself, after living with this statement for many months and using it in many different connections, I do not see implied in it the distinctions that the critic sees. Jesus Christ is inseparable from God's self-disclosure and in-separable from his seeking love. Revelation is not complete without Jesus Christ, and the gospel is nonexistent without him. On the other hand, it would be a mistake to say that God does not reveal himself where, when, and as he chooses. Per-haps the clue to a solution to the difficulty is that many theolo-gians have seen the Christ, but not always the historical Jesus, wherever God has revealed himself or wherever he now reveals himself. But the full meaning of that revelation, the full reality of that Christ, is not evident without definitive reference to Jesus Christ. This principle applies equally well to Biblical interpretation, contemporary preaching, or any evidence of Christ in our midst.

The term "objective" is used in referring to this statement of purpose. As pointed out before, a policy statement like this, intended as a guide to the whole process, appears to be more useful as objective than other kinds of analyses referred to as objectives.

Whose objective is this? It is the objective of the Christian educator, whether he be the one who prepares curriculum suggestions for the church at large, the teacher, the pupil, the parent, the church, the friend, the neighbor, the husband, or the wife. In all cases, it is a basic guide to what is again a continuing communicative transaction, a continuity of experience in the light of the gospel, a growing awareness and a more faithful response.

PROCESS

How does the communicative transaction take place in Christian education? What is the clue to process and method? Learning, in effect, involves all the factors discussed under the question of the behavioral sciences. It is a matter of the development of personality through the gaining and refining of experience, a matter of the use and transformation of motives. It calls for discriminating use of the varieties of learning processes, takes place in accordance with the patterns of human growth and development, and is deeply influenced by the culture, the society, and the groups of which the individual is a member.

Teaching is the guidance of learning. Thus, teaching the Christian faith and the Christian life is, in fact, a matter of inviting persons into meaningful participation in the life of the worshiping, witnessing, and working community of persons in Christ (implying the individual as well as corporate aspects of membership). This is the process of Christian education—

the deepest participation, engagement, involvement in the
life and work of the Christian community.

For Christian education, participation in the life and work
of the community of faith implies participation in certain
key activities of the fellowship:

The community studies the Bible, doctrine, history, and
contemporary affairs; the learner is invited to "know the
truth" through participation in that study.

The community worships; the learner is invited to participate in that worship, to adore, repent, consider, and go
forth in commitment. He is invited to participate in a public
worship that is both personal and truly social, and in a private
worship that plumbs the depths and scales the heights of
experience.

The community acts in witness, service, and social action;
the learner is invited to participate in that action. He is asked
to practice what he believes, knowing that faith leads to service, that service tests faith, and that service leads to faith.
Missions, welfare, public responsibility, personal helpfulness,
and social and economic reconstruction are all involved.

The community expresses itself creatively in music, the
spoken word, literature, liturgy, drama, architecture, and the
other arts; the learner is invited not only to listen to this
expression but himself to participate in the creative expression
of faith in and with the community.

The community lives as a fellowship of love, inwardly
through the life of the group (the sharing of ideas and feelings,
even playing together), and outwardly through the invitation
to fellowship extended to all; the learner is invited to participate in this fellowship of love. "That we may have fellowship . . . fellowship with the Father and with his Son Jesus
Christ . . . the completeness of joy."

The community practices stewardship through its use of

its resources and through the working out of its individual and corporate vocation; the learner is invited to participate in this stewardship.

Participation in such ways in the life and work of the Christian community prompts needs, raises questions, presents problems, and encourages interests. At the same time the resources for fulfillment are at hand in the community, the body of Christ, of which one is a member. The key to learning in this community is the undertaking of appropriate tasks: acting, with the resources, in the light of needs, questions, problems, and interests.

I must act; learning requires self-activity. But at the same time that self-activity takes place in relation to the self-activity of God, the teacher, the community, the church, and the home. This is the complexity of the communicative transaction. Yet without the learner's self-activity, without his undertaking appropriate tasks, learning does not take place.

What are the tasks? The very specific task or cluster of tasks upon which I am working at any given time is symbolized by group and individual goals. Any goal or specific task that is appropriate to Christian education, however, will be integrally related to one or more of the following learning tasks:

Making contact with the field of relationships—in the light of the gospel.

Exploring the field of relationships—in the light of the gospel.

Discovering meaning and value in the field of relationships —in the light of the gospel.

Appropriating that meaning and value personally.

Assuming responsibility, personal and social, in the field of relationships—in the light of the gospel.

In the light of the gospel. . . . There must be a lifelong listening, a listening with growing awareness, to the gospel, and response in faith and love. This listening and response will themselves require making contact, exploration, discovery of meaning and value, and assumption of responsibility.

Christian education assumes that a grasp of the field of relationships is being achieved by the individual through his experiences in school, at home, in the neighborhood, and elsewhere. The corollary assumption is that inviting and assisting the learner to undertake the learning tasks *in the light of the gospel* is the definitive role of Christian education. The direct implication, then, is that for Christian education the prime task is that of listening with growing alertness to the gospel and responding in faith and love.

Misgivings are sometimes voiced about the appropriateness of this interpretation of the process of Christian education as it applies to children. We need to be clear that the relationship of the child to the church is a very close one, especially as regards participating in the worship, witness, and work of the church. The close relationship is possible because of the organic unity of the Christian family and the fact that the child may feel himself to be a real contributor to the life of the people of God. His contribution is, of course, in terms of activities that are important and real to him—playing, working, exploring, talking, praying, giving, and worshiping. Yet there is no essential expression of the life and work of the church in which he cannot have some sense of participation. In fact, children would find the church a much more exciting and challenging fellowship if such participation were permitted.

Participation in the Christian mission provides an excellent example of the meaning of the process of Christian education. Education in mission, as in any other kind of education, lacks Christian meaning unless it moves within the context of God's reconciling work on man's behalf. Education in mission, however, participates in the aim of seeing things as they are and coming to grips with life. Thus it implies informed, skilled, and reflective involvement in the work of the church and the world at every level. Without education in mission, the individual and the group are left far short of seeing things as they are and are ill equipped to come to grips with life.

In the context of such involvement bearing witness to Christ by word and deed takes on meaning. Our bearing witness becomes a ministry of the community of reconciliation. Being members of such a community means that we are on a mission. We are in a church that is on a mission, a mission without which the church would not be the church of Jesus Christ.

This is how mission is involved in the education of the Christian. In order to be a Christian he has to be introduced to and accept the mission of the church; in order to validate his membership he must participate to the utmost in the fulfilling of the church's mission.

A number of difficult questions, all of them grist for a meaningful theory of Christian education, are introduced by such a view. One such problem is that there is a standard missionary program of the church, a vast enterprise at home and abroad, known as "missions." In most respects it qualifies as an essential part of the mission of reconciliation of the church of Jesus Christ. In some respects it does not. All would agree that it must be understood and evaluated honestly and appreciatively, that every member of Christ's body must feel a personal responsibility for it, that it must be augmented and rendered effective in many ways, and that it cannot be equated with "the Christian mission."

A second problem is that of ecumenics, where one might almost say that "mission" and "unity" are the watchwords. The ecumenical movement is one where the church of Jesus Christ is "finding itself" in terms functional to the changing conditions and needs of the mid-twentieth-century world. Are we listening intently to what it says mission means in this world at this time?

A third area of concern is social education and action. This is bearing witness! Here are the consciences of the individual member and the church at work upon the knotty problems of human relations and social righteousness at their very doorstep. This is clearly mission, and many more need to take it seriously enough to engage in it effectively.

A fourth problem is that we are faced with a constant danger in our motive and approach to mission. The facts starkly challenge our prevailing notions and attitudes: (1) Mission is rooted in the involvement in sin, which we share with all humanity, and which creates an inescapable mutual responsibility that knows no social barriers or limits. (2) Mission is the ministry of the word—which defines its one basic ingredient. (3) Mission is not really a cheerful set of projects in world friendship. Is not the mission of Christ's people to participate in his life, his suffering, his death, and his rising again, that the sin of the world may be taken away? The point in world friendship is to gain real understanding of and real identification with those with whom our lives and destinies are bound up, but whom we do not even know. In today's world the joy of such friendship cannot help being deeply touched with pain. (4) Mission is vocation. This used to mean something quite clear and definite: certain persons called to be missionaries. It still means that, but it also means much more, since every member of Christ's body is called to mission.

A wise piece of statesmanship decided that the dissemination of the information on missions necessary to gain widespread support for the enterprise would be done in the form of education. As we and the learners we serve grapple with the kinds of problems that have just been listed, the nature of the church will become apparent, the mission of Christ's church will become clear, the church will join hands with its missionary enterprise in understanding and support, the missionary enterprise itself will take on new meaning and direction, and the individual member will grow in Christian self-realization through the indispensably enlightening experiences of involvement.

Participation applies to everyone, clergy and laity alike. Reporting on an inner-city church, Truman B. Douglass quotes the ministers as saying, "We had to *earn* the right to serve the people of this community. So 'participation' became the key word." His report continues:

> The ministers found rooms in the tenement area and lived there—those who were married with their families. Every member of the Parish was pledged to be an active member of at least one social or political organization working for the improvement of the neighborhood. This involved the staff in such activities as the enforcement of tenement laws, an attack on rat infestation, improvement of ambulance service to slum neighborhoods, work with youthful drug addicts, establishing friendly relations with leaders of teen-age gangs, and understanding the political structure of a metropolitan area, and the improvement of housing and health. (*Harper's Magazine,* November, 1958.)

These then are some of the implications of education through participation in the life of the worshiping, witnessing, working community of Christians. The group and individual goals that are implied provide the skeleton of the curriculum. In other words, the curriculum, the plan for teaching-learning situations, consists of a sequence of goals and activities, oriented to the key activities of the fellowship as expressions of the learning tasks, undertaken by individuals and groups.

The specific methods of Christian education (reading, lecture, discussion, drama, audio-visual, group dynamics, singing, art activities, field trips, prayer, church attendance, etc.) are ways, adapted to the needs and interests of the pupil, for his participation to become richer, more meaningful, and more effective.

THE ORGANIZING PRINCIPLE OF THE CURRICULUM

Christian education is the church's concern for the person as he grows and develops and is therefore chiefly involved with the "live" communicating of the Christian faith. Such live communication requires integrity and understandability on the part of the church and responsibility and appropriation on the part of the person.

But the matter of organizing a curriculum as a medium for live communication has its problems. We are bothered that we feel our failure in the areas of study, creative expression, action, fellowship, stewardship, and worship; that we feel that we have not really communicated in the church or the neighborhood or beyond our circle; and that we sense a lack of relevance to the modern mind, the modern world, and the modern soul.

Because of lack of perspective, perhaps we have mistaken our task. Perhaps our business is evangelism, communication with the emphasis on decisive encounter. This, of course, is our task in Christian education, providing we see it as communication that is a kind of lifelong evangelism. Lifelong evangelism is a matter of perceiving the gospel, accepting the gospel, and discovering and fulfilling the gospel's demands upon us.

Furthermore, we are compelled to raise the question of communication—to whom? Can we be content to communicate "within" the Christian community? Thus we face the problems of the nature of our communication and the object of our communication, in order to approach the matter of organizing a curriculum that will help in the process of communication.

The curriculum is a plan for communicating the gospel, based upon the best answers we can give to these questions:

To whom are we speaking?

What is their "listening situation?"

What do we have to say?

Who are *we*?

As we review the principles that have already been discussed, the clues to communication begin to be evident: (1) Communication depends upon our being the church, living its life, and doing its work. (2) Communication depends upon the learner's responsible participation. (3) Communication depends upon creating a climate for acceptance and achievement, encouraging the creative, and helping the person to communicate back from where he stands. (4) Communication depends upon our recognizing that *we* are really nobody much but that we find ourselves together doing strange things the meaning of which the Scriptures explain to us.

How, then, do you work out a curriculum plan with all this in mind? How do you organize Christian education? Is there some dependable organizing principle to use?

The organizing principle serves the essential function of bridging the gap between the scope of Christian education and the actual learning situation. The organizing principle is the clue to the design of the curriculum. Because the design is a matter of creating learning situations that will implement the process of Christian education, it is necessary for the organizing principle to reflect the process clearly, focus the scope of Christian education unmistakably toward the objective, and be an integral expression of Christian education's working within the context of the life of the community of persons in Christ. The function the organizing principle must serve properly is to put all these understandings in order for curriculum purposes and thus to tell us what we need to know in order to proceed with setting up the learning situations that constitute the curriculum.

Two standard ways have been found of coming at an organizing principle: (1) We may ask how to use the substance of the church's teaching so as to give promise of the person's realizing the purpose of Christian education. (2) We may ask what principle shall be used to decide on the continuity for the curriculum.

In either case, the items that need clarification and discussion are the substance of the church's teaching, the process of personal realization of the purpose of Christian education, and the question of continuity (sequence, progression) in curriculum.

The major solution required is between the demands of logical and psychological continuity. If the substance of the church's teaching is the important thing, then continuity tends to be logical. If personal realization is the important thing, then continuity tends to be psychological.

Very few would advocate a clear-cut choice between logical and psychological continuity. Most Christian educators recognize that both elements must be included and handled with integrity. Generally, three questions may be asked to test the adequacy and validity of any proposed organizing principle: Does this organizing principle treat the scope of Christian education thoroughly and with integrity? Does this principle promise the effective realization of the objective? Does it really tell us what we need to know in order to proceed with setting up the curriculum?

The specific tension in Christian education is between the demands of the faith and the church and the requirements and situation of the learner. The organizing principle that has been used by Protestant educators for some time and that placed the emphasis upon the requirements and situation of the learner, came out of the Study of Christian Education:

> The organizing principle of the curriculum, from the view-
> point of the Christian gospel, is to be found in the changing
> needs and experiences of the individual as these include his
> relation to (1) God, as revealed in Jesus Christ; (2) his fellow
> men and human society; (3) his place in the work of the world;
> (4) the Christian fellowship, the church; (5) the continuous
> process of history, viewed as a carrier of the divine purpose and
> revealer of the moral law; (6) the universe in all its wonder
> and complexity. (Paul H. Vieth, *The Church and Christian
> Education,* pp. 145–146.)

This is the organizing principle cited in *A Guide for Curriculum in Christian Education* (p. 30). The significance of the principle is threefold: (1) It states that everything that is done in the curriculum is an experience of some sort and that constant attention must be given to what is happening in the pupil's mind, heart, and soul. (2) It points out that in order to help the pupil meet his changing needs and mature in his changing experience the scope of Christian education must be kept before him in various appropriate ways. (3) It makes clear that it is the gospel that confronts the individual in all these vital relationships and makes every response of his possible.

In such an organizing principle, subject matter and experience are inseparable, and experience is the first consideration in curriculum planning. At the same time, there is a danger of disorganization and anarchy in curriculum planning if individual experience is used as the organizing principle. The crucial question may be raised by asking whether "In relation to—" and the analysis of a set of significant relationships guarantee the fundamental organization that curriculum requires.

At this point it will be useful to look at organizing principles stated or implied in various denominational documents:

UNITED PRESBYTERIAN: *Basic Principles,* 1947.
If one must speak of a center for curriculum, then it is truest to say that Christ is the center—Christ as we know him only through the Scriptures of the Old and New Testaments, Christ the eternal Word of God. But Christ is unwilling to be at the center alone. He takes the child into the center with him, so that no one can have him at the center without having the child there also. The child must be understood in the light of Christ's relationship to him and his relationship to Christ, never in isolation from Christ as though the nature of his needs and problems were self-evident. (P. 17.)

The all-inclusive principle of training for active discipleship will not be adequately provided for by occasional units in the curriculum, but must govern constantly the approach to the total work of teaching. (P. 8.)

PROTESTANT EPISCOPAL: *Preview*, 1958–1959.
The objective is *response*. The time is *now*. The place is *the lives of our people*, both those who learn and those who teach.

METHODIST: *Foundations of Christian Teaching in Methodist Churches*, 1960.
(The curriculum provides) particular types of experiences that, it is hoped, will bring the pupil into the presence of God and encourage him to respond to God in faith, love, and understanding.

LUTHERAN: *The Functional Objectives for Christian Education*, 1959.
The God-man relationship is a dynamic one which occurs within the context of life; learning is most effective and meaningful when it is related to the pupil's ongoing experience; the curriculum is the way in which the educational agency provides for significant learning experiences; curriculum is most helpful when it assists the individual in his own integration of his learning experiences. If these things are true, it would follow that the curriculum should be designed in a way that will enable the learner to grasp the relevance of the Word of God to his experiences and to appreciate the way in which his total life is bound up with his relationship to God. At every stage of life persons are deeply involved in events and concerns which make them receptive to the Word and provide unique opportunities to learn.

One of the problems in organizing the curriculum, however, is the question of whether each learner and his experiences are so unique that they bear no resemblance to other individuals and their experiences. If this were the case, a special educational program would have to be tailored for each person. Fortunately this is not true. While every person possesses individual differences, many of the most significant aspects of life lie in the realm of common experience. By virtue of being a member of the society in which he lives, the individual becomes involved in many situations, faces many demands and responsibilities which are essentially the same as those faced by others. These situations become recurrent opportunities for learning throughout life, for once they have become a part of the experience of the individual, they tend to arise continually in new and more complex configurations. For educational purposes it is possible to identify these common areas of experience and utilize them as continuing strands in the development of curriculum.

Life involvements in themselves are essentially neutral. They are the ground or context within which learnings may occur, but they do not constitute desired learnings in themselves. In Christian education significant learning takes place when the individual is confronted in these situations with the Word of God. (Pp. 20–21.)

PRESBYTERIAN U.S.: "Golden Paper," July, 1958.
The organizing principle of the curriculum is the church's offering to persons in the situation in which they stand the Bible and the life of the church, the covenant community, as both witness to and instrument of God's revelation of himself to man.

UNITED CHURCH OF CHRIST: *A Statement of Educational Principles,* 1957.
Through the continuum of experience each growing person can identify himself with the fellowship and share its purposes, its worship, its beliefs, its work, and the fruits of the Spirit, which it seeks to foster and support.

UNITED CHURCH OF CANADA: "Curriculum: Its Organizing Principle, Plan, and Unit Descriptions," July 3, 1959.
The curriculum of Christian education may be organized by providing systematic opportunities for persons to be confronted with the gospel in the Christian community.

Obviously, the organizing principle is being considerably rethought. Two guideposts to this rethinking appear to be particularly important: (1) The insights and values of "experience in relation to—" are being conserved. Curriculum is to be organized around the moving and developing expeience of the individual and the group. (2) Use is to be made of the experience of the church. The curriculum may be organized in terms of the experience of the fellowship of believers. This may be the means of focusing significant experience for Christian education.

In the light of the present insights, the reformulation of the

144 Theory and Design of Christian Education

organizing principle will involve the dynamics (experience) of individual and corporate association with, and membership in, the community of persons in Christ. The following is suggested as such an organizing principle:

The curriculum of Christian education may be organized by planning to involve learners, with all their varied needs and developing experience, in the church's ongoing study, worship, action, creative expression, fellowship, and stewardship—in which they are helped to come face to face with the gospel through study of the Bible and through the life of devotion; see the relevance of the gospel to the understanding of all of life—God, man, nature, and history; accept the promises and implications of the Christian faith; and become committed to membership in the worshiping, witnessing, working community of persons in Christ and to full discipleship in the world.

This statement of the organizing principle depends upon the concept that learning takes place through involvement. Such involvement, if it is to lead to Christian learning, definitely implies the learner's participating in a personal way in the very life and work of the community. For curriculum purposes this means undertaking the Christian learning tasks through which the life and work of the community find expression and through which the Christian faith and life may be known and appropriated.

One of the implications of this organizing principle is that the church must become in reality a "primary" social group. Its members must do more real living together and enter upon their mission with new motivation and imaginative daring.

Does this organizing principle use the principle of scope thoroughly and with integrity? The individual's business, the world's business, and the church's business is with God, man, the natural world, and history. As the church lives its life and does its work, drawing persons individually and corporately into association and membership, the scope of Christian educa-

tion is required to come into play. The scope of Christian
education and the major concerns of the church are one and
the same.

Does this organizing principle promise to realize the objective effectively? Awareness and response begin with association with the worshiping, witnessing, working community, are
realized in membership in that community, and come to ever
more mature fulfillment as the person and the group seek to
become effective instruments for the continuation of God's
work of reconciliation in Christ. One of the chief aims of the
curriculum is to help toward unity of individual and corporate
experience in Christ—the movement of the person in Christ
through self-realization to full and effective realization of
personality, so that true wholeness becomes possible. Throughout, Christian education seeks that all experience, individual
and corporate, may be in Christ, that Christ shall be the core
of personal integrity, and that the experience of the home,
the church's educational program, and other agencies, may
contribute to this experience. Under these circumstances
awareness of the gospel and response to it may lead, not by
means of human agency alone, to self-acceptance and courage,
and thus to unity of experience in Christ. The heart of the
matter, again, is the church's faithfulness to its real task.

Does this organizing principle really tell us what we need
to know in order to proceed with setting up the curriculum?
The curriculum organized in accordance with this principle,
while departing from many of our present curricular plans
and customs, may nevertheless be visualized quite clearly. To
the extent that we are able to see the life of the community
of persons in Christ and the meaning of participation in that
community's life and work, we are able to see the shape of
the curriculum. The Christian learning tasks would be undertaken by the individual and the group, primarily in the form
of the activities of the church: study, worship, creative expression, action, fellowship, and stewardship. All these experiences
would be included in the total educational life of the in-

dividual and the group. They would take appropriate form in
any given situation in accordance with the needs and capacities
of the learner or learners. The church would decide what its
real tasks were, and the ways in which various persons and
groups might be invited to assume responsibilities for those
tasks. Undertaking these responsibilities would lead to the
gaining and expressing of ideas, values, beliefs, behaviors,
commitments, and habits that were Christian and that had
integrity for the person and the group.

THE ORGANIZING MEDIUM OF THE CURRICULUM

How may the organizing principle be specifically implemented in curriculum design? What medium shall be used to
organize the curriculum? The proposal, growing out of the
preceding consideration of principles, is that the Christian
learning tasks be the organizing medium for the curriculum.

The learning tasks are an expression of a valid approach to
learning, to the teaching-learning process, well grounded in
educational theory and in theology. Some of the principles that
have been discussed and support this claim are the following:

Learning is a process of human becoming, through experience, in a comprehensive field of relationships.

Human becoming, including Christian becoming, is both
a personal and interpersonal process.

Becoming is based on the assumption of responsibility (ability and willingness to respond in appropriate ways to the
opportunities for meaningful and helpful relationships). Thus
the concept of tasks, enterprises, or responsibilities to be
undertaken is required.

The gospel defines the field of relationships in a way that
otherwise would not be obvious or available. Thus the prime
task is listening and responding to the gospel.

Our way of becoming involves cycles of exploring the field
of relationships, discovering meaning and value in it, and
appropriating that meaning and value personally.

Human becoming, including Christian becoming, involves

the development of personality, which may be defined in terms of the categories of meaning and value. (I become what I mean to myself; I become what I value.)

True becoming involves conversion in the light of the gospel.

The chronology of the experience of human becoming involves the occurrence and recurrence of the processes of human becoming (spiraling cycles of exploration, discovery, and appropriation, undergirded by the assumption of responsibility, and given distinctive orientation and character by constant attention and response to the gospel).

The essentially personal nature of the learning tasks has been described by Robert Redfield, in *The Educational Experience:* "I see a movement of the mind that begins as a free reaching outward, impelled by curiosity, wonder, excitement. I see the mind next pass through a sort of contest, a conversation of alternatives or between this event and that idea, in fruitful interaction. And then, if education happens, there is a third phase of the cycle in which the new fact or idea of experience is made part of me; I act, internally, with regard to it." (P. 14.)

The essentially interpersonal nature of the learning tasks has been described by Maurice Friedman, in his article, "Martin Buber's 'Theology' and Religious Education," making clear both its human and divine dimensions:

> Religious education, as Martin Buber sees it, should not be concerned with imparting objective information about God's being, but with pointing man to the age-old, ever-new dialogue with the God who hides and reveals himself. The way in which this education takes place is itself a dialogue—between man and man.
>
> Dialogue is not intellectual dialectic but the real meeting and full personal interchange in the course of lived life between two persons each of whom allows the other to exist as an independent "other" and not just as a content of his own experience or an object to be placed in his mental categories.

> Religious education is "mutual contact, . . . the genuinely
> reciprocal meeting in the fullness of life between one active
> existence and another" and faith is entering into this reci-
> procity, binding oneself in relationship "with an undemon-
> strable and unprovable, yet even so, in relationship, know-
> able Being, from whom all meaning comes."

If this treatment of the learning tasks is correct, then the
curriculum of Christian education consists in individuals and
groups carrying on the learning tasks in the context of the
Christian community. The tasks are the guides to involvement
in the church's ongoing study, worship, action, creative expression, fellowship, and stewardship. They provide the ed-
ucationally and theologically valid medium for Christian
education through such participation and involvement.

The organizing principle is a statement of the way in which
the scope of Christian education may be used to accomplish
the objective. The learning tasks, in turn, provide the guides
to the concrete activities implied in the organizing principle.
They implement the organizing principle directly and thus
become an "organizing medium."

This is particularly important to the curriculum planner
and builder, since his chief concern is to suggest group and
individual goals that may guide individuals and groups to
outcomes that are related to the objective. If the group and
individual goals he suggests are carefully selected aspects of
the Christian learning tasks as expressions of the organizing
principle, then the integral connection with the whole context,
scope, purpose, and process of Christian education has been
established.

How may the learning tasks act as the organizing medium?
The curricular function of learning tasks is to join personal
and group motivations to the scope of Christian education.
The result, skeletal to the curriculum, will be group and
individual goals that imply the necessary and appropriate
educational activities.

The joining of personal and group motivations and the

scope of Christian education in terms of its context is the joining of experience and content in the setting of the Christian community. Thus in group and individual goals, educational activity and subject matter are mated in a dynamic setting.

Traditionally, subject matter and experience have been separated in curriculum thinking. When the pupil passed through the door of the school we tended to think of him as leaving his life experience behind and entering the world of subject matter. This was impossible, however, since the moment he came into the situation he brought his life experience with him. Furthermore, the life of the school itself consisted of myriad experiences. But every effort was made to forget that this was the case and to concentrate on subject matter.

In the church school the pupil was thought of as entering the world of the Bible, Christian doctrine, and church history. Even the experience of conversion and evangelism was often left to those outside the church school and was not thought of as part of the curriculum. If this were so in the case of such an obvious life experience as conversion, how much more were other types of life experience excluded from the curriculum.

The outlook has changed, and it is now recognized that subject matter and experience are tied up together in a very close way. They are tied together because the way to learn subject matter is to experience it. The life of David is religious subject matter. How does one come to know it? Through hearing about David, seeing pictures of him, reading his life story, tracing the locale of his exploits, considering the significance of his life and experience, and telling the story to other people. Hearing, seeing, reading, tracing, considering, and telling are experiences.

Experience and subject matter are also tied together, because experience is poor and thin unless it is rooted in rich and fertile subject matter. How do I make a choice in life? This is the consideration of life experience. My answer, however, is bound to be flimsy unless I am reading the important books on the subject (including the Bible), listening to what experienced people have to say on it, and giving consideration to some of the films on the subject. Books, the Bible, other people's experience, and films are subject matter.

What sorts of experience shall be selected to comprise the curriculum? Active experience is expressed grammatically by "ing." This is what goes on in the curriculum. People do things, reflect on what they do (which is a form of doing), and learn from that doing and reflection. Just to indicate the scope of experiencing as it takes place in the curriculum, here are a few of the "ings" that will be found:

Growing	Taking action	Touching	Knowing
Understanding	Perceiving	Developing	Becoming
Needing	Conceptualiz-	Appreciating	Equipping
Wanting	ing	Sensing	Reorganizing
Teaching	Remembering	Succeeding	Healing
Collecting	Looking	Accomplishing	Evangelizing
Speaking	Recreating	Designing	Using
Accepting	Joining	Studying	Hearing
Considering	Creating	Singing	Following
Imagining	Talking	Thinking	Seeing
Reading	Witnessing	Worshiping	Feeling
Generalizing	Giving	Believing	Purposing
Selecting	Urging	Seeking	Yielding
Sharing	Relating	Meditating	Training
Forgiving	Showing	Loving	Insisting
Guessing	Challenging	Planning	Organizing
Surrendering	Rejecting	Traveling	Communing
Discovering	Changing	Practicing	Preaching
Realizing	Weighing	Belonging	Waiting
Adapting	Analyzing	Working	Going
Exploring	Writing	Dancing	Expressing
Playing	Learning	Kneeling	Memorizing
Praying	Listening	Bowing	Partaking
Deciding	Serving	Motivating	Obeying

By way of illustration, the teaching of controversial issues, training alert Christian citizens (the church's social action), calls for the following activities:

Recognizing, defining, exploring, and analyzing the issue.
Suggesting possible solutions.
Collecting and recording data.
Presenting and evaluating data.
Testing hypotheses.
Determining possible conclusions.

For education, however, not all activities are experiences of equal value. A serious attempt must be made to determine the basic experience categories of education, around which all other educational activities may cluster and to which they contribute. It is this challenge to rigorous and comprehensive categorization of educational activities that has led to the formulation of the basic learning tasks:

Making contact with the field of relationships.
Exploring the field of relationships.
Discovering meaning and value in the field of relationships.
Appropriating that meaning and value personally.
Assuming personal and social responsibility.

The whole process of perception, conceptualization, and the sharing of general human experience is summed up in these learning tasks.

But the learning tasks of Christian education are pointed up in terms of a distinctive orientation that is defined by the scope of Christian education: the whole field of relationships *in the light of the gospel*. Thus the distinctive learning task for Christian education is that of listening with growing alertness to the gospel and responding in faith and love. Around this task cluster a number of activities: Taking part in the worship, life, and work of the church; studying the Bible in order to know the gospel; praying; repenting in the light of the gospel, accepting the gospel, receiving the gospel, depending upon the gospel, growing in realization of the implications and demands of the gospel; reviewing, re-examining, and reconstructing discoveries and personal appropriations of meaning and value in the light of the gospel. (From *The Objective of Christian Education for Senior High Young People*.)

This learning task provides the basis for the emotional learnings that underlie Christian experience, such as faith and devotion to righteousness, truth, mercy, forgiveness, and love. It acquaints the individual with those sorts of general experience which are most likely to have religious implications, such as history, art, and civic and international affairs. The person is introduced to the distinctively Christian aspects of experience, such as the Bible, hymnody, doctrine, and missions. This task also provides the basis for appropriate commitments at the various levels of experience, such as love of the church, response to the gospel, discipleship, and vocation; and it encourages the development of deliberation, reflection, insight, prayer, and worship.

In order that the focus may be on participation in the life the church lives and the work it does, listening with growing alertness to the gospel and responding in faith and love will most often, then, take the form of engagement in the community's study, worship, action, creative expression, fellowship, and stewardship.

Clearly a learning task is not simply an activity. To be meaningful, the activity must be inseparably bound up with an object. Group and individual goals, as has been said, represent in themselves (as do the learning tasks) a mating of an effective activity with a meaningful object. This is what makes them useful for curriculum. To illustrate group and individual goals, take the following few:

Comparing the Gospels.
Designing a stained-glass window.

Raising the youth budget.
Finding out about international affairs.
Discussing local candidates.
Remembering and anticipating history.
Visiting a mission.
Analyzing an exhibit of religious art.
Reconciling divergent views.
Coming into communicant membership.
Partaking of the sacraments.

Constellations of goals and activities group themselves at various levels. In some cases they correspond to age levels. In other cases they do not. But they do define experience levels. Take the case of maturity, for instance. A constellation of goals and activities characteristic of maturity might use such "ings" as:

Understanding	Creating	Giving	Seeking
Witnessing	Worshiping	Realizing	Meditating
Sharing	Believing	Taking action	Planning
Praying	Loving	Working	Organizing
Remembering	Purposing	Evangelizing	etc.
Knowing	Reorganizing	Studying	
Appreciating	Teaching	Thinking	

Sequence of goals and activities are also indispensable to the curriculum. This means coming to grips, step by step, through various levels with various aspects of the field of relationships, experiencing them more fully and meaningfully. For instance, some such sequence as this might be applicable to the Bible:

Discovering, seeing, and hearing the Bible.
Reading, analyzing, weighing, understanding, appreciating, and memorizing the Bible.
Believing, accepting, loving, and using the Bible.
Sharing, witnessing to, and teaching the Bible.

Notice in this connection how closely this analysis parallels the tasks of making contact, exploring, discovering meaning and value, appropriating meaning and value, and assuming responsibility. This bears out the probability that there is in the learning tasks not only a sharp definition of the basic modes of educational experience but also a clue to educational sequence.

As an organizing medium, then, the learning tasks provide a practical way of translating the scope of Christian education into goals and activities that spell out the process of Christian education. Their educational validity is indicated by their usefulness in connection with guiding and directing experience. Their theological validity is indicated by their affinity to the scope of Christian education. They directly implement the organizing principle and are susceptible to analysis in terms of levels of educational experience and sequences of educational experience.

As a summary illustration of the role of the learning tasks as the organizing medium for the curriculum, let us take the two approaches to the scope of Christian education that are usually considered to be in tension in the curriculum. The first approach is that of the church. As it views the scope of Christian education it sees it in terms of its major concerns (viewed both as content and as experience): the word of God, the theological task, what the church is and does, the church in history, the church in today's world, human relations, the realization of the self, and the Christian life. The church knows that its task is not done unless Christian education curriculum deals with these concerns seriously and thoroughly.

On the other hand, the second approach is that of the learner, with his personal, existential concerns. He also approaches the scope of Christian education, the whole field of relationships, in terms of content and experience, but his major concerns are (in Erikson's terms) the achievement of a sense of trust, a sense of autonomy, a sense of initiative, a sense of industry, a sense of identity, a sense of intimacy, a sense of creativity, and a sense of integrity. He knows that the curriculum of Christian education will either help him at these points or prove to be hopelessly irrelevant.

The way for the learner to achieve his ends is to make contact with the field of relationships, explore it, discover its meaning and value personally, and assume personal and social responsibility. In so doing there is hope of achieving the sense of trust, autonomy, initiative, and the rest of his needs. There is even more hope of doing so if he undertakes these tasks in the light of the gospel, thus engaging throughout in the task of listening with growing alertness to the gospel and responding in faith and love. Thus his sense of trust, autonomy, initiative, and the rest of his needs become related to the word of God, the theological task, what the church is and does, and the rest of the church's concerns.

Since they are the church's concerns, the learner finds himself, in undertaking these tasks, engaging in the activities and seeking the goals that are characteristic of the community of worship, witness, and work. He will involve himself in studying, worshiping and praying, witnessing, engaging in service, taking appropriate social action, expressing the Christian faith creatively, engaging in the fellowship of the common life, participating in the outreach of mission, and practicing stewardship.

These, in turn, will take the form of a variety and range of specific group and individual goals and activities, arranged most often in a sequence of contact, exploration, discovery, appropriation, and responsibility.

SUMMARY

The principles of context, scope, purpose, process, the organizing principle, and the organizing medium for the curriculum of Christian education may be summarized in two statements in juxtaposition to each other. One involves the educational process; the other involves the distinctive elements in Christian education. Once these statements are made, in relation to each other, they may be analyzed in terms of the principles that have been discussed.

The Educational Process	*Distinctive Elements in Christian Education*
Establishing relationships;	Listening with growing alertness to the gospel;
Exploring the field of relationships;	
Discovering meaning and value in the field of relationships;	
Appropriating that meaning and value personally;	Responding in faith and love;
Assuming personal and social responsibility:	
—through personal involvement in the processes of society and culture.	—through personal involvement in the life and work of the people of God.

While the context of education is society and culture, the context of Christian education is the life and work of the people of God.

While the scope of education is the field of relationships, the scope of Christian education is the field of relationships in the light of the gospel. Thus the scope includes both society and culture and the life and work of the people of God.

The purpose of Christian education is to help persons to be aware of God's self-disclosure and seeking love in Jesus Christ and to respond in faith and love (directly implemented by the distinctive elements in Christian education).

The process of education is personal involvement in the processes of society and culture, implemented by establishing relationships, exploring the field of relationships, discovering meaning and value in it, appropriating that meaning and value personally, and assuming personal and social responsibility. The basic social and psychological condition for education is the personal involvement in the processes of society and culture that requires the assumption of personal and social responsibility. The sequence of education is the establishing of relationships, the exploration, the discovery, the personal appropriation, and the assumption of responsibility that are built into the learning tasks.

The process of Christian education adds the involvement and task that changes the whole orientation of education. The basic social and psychological condition of education is met, but also in terms of personal involvement in the life and work of the people of God. The sequence of education is still relied on but also in terms of listening with growing alertness to the gospel and responding in faith and love.

The organizing principle of the curriculum of education is the processes of society and culture; the organizing principle of the curriculum of Christian education is the processes of the life and work of the people of God.

The organizing medium for the curriculum is the learning tasks, combining the educational process and the distinctive elements in Christian education.

If the organizing *principle* is to be understood, then the answers to these questions must be clear: What is the worshiping, witnessing, working community of the people of God? What are its functions and responsibilities? What opportunities, problems, and challenges is it presently facing? What, then, are its life and work, in the light of its nature, functions, responsibilities, and present opportunities, problems, and challenges?

If the organizing *medium* is to be used effectively, then the answers to these questions must be clear: What does involvement in the life and work of the community of the people of God mean? What does involvement in its life and work mean for individuals, congregations, families, age-level groups, and other groups? The answers to these questions are the clue to curriculum design.

Design

Design...

THE DESIGN OF THE CURRICULUM OF CHRISTIAN EDUCATION IS A matter of creating a learning situation that will implement the process of Christian education. Design means deciding on sequences of activities and experiences by which the learning tasks may be effectively undertaken by individuals and groups.

Individuality and flexibility of design are necessary and are possible because of the definiteness of the context, scope, purpose, and process. Only when these are unclear does design become necessarily rigid. A fluid curriculum may be achieved if there is one well understood over-all objective, and if proximate goals in harmony with the objective are set co-operatively by the learning group and its leaders.

Having dealt with the four basic principles of Christian education and its curriculum, it is possible to lay a firm foundation for curriculum design in terms of an organizing principle and the medium for the implementation of that organizing principle. We turn now to the two specific implications of these principles that spell out the basic practicalities of the curriculum: sequence and flexibility. These are dealt with in Chapter 6. The questions are: How may sequence be determined? How may different educational settings, a variety of methods, and individual, community, and cultural differences be taken into account realistically? How may specific learning situations be planned and guided?

Chapter 7 discusses the question of the development and use of curriculum materials. Materials are seen in the form of the curriculum guide, the area guide, the resource unit, the teaching-learning unit, and other aids. The place of evaluation in the curriculum is explored. The responsibilities of various parties to the curriculum are dealt with: the individual, the group, the family, the local parish, community agencies, the denomination, and interdenominational agencies.

The curriculum is intended as an aid to the person, the group, and the church in the teaching-learning process; yet they are also the parties to its construction. Communication of a "live" sort takes place where the person is, in groups, in the church, with the world. This then is where the curriculum is built and where it does its work.

Chapter 6

PLANNING FOR SEQUENCE
AND FLEXIBILITY

H OW MAY SEQUENCE and flexibility be achieved in the curriculum? The achievement of sequence is a matter of progression and continuity. Flexibility means taking differences seriously: differences in educational settings, differences in method, and differences among individuals, communities, and cultures.

SEQUENCE

What are the sequential steps by which a person grasps, uses, and participates in the whole field of relationships in the light of the gospel? The clue to sequence in Christian education is in the context, the process, and the learning tasks, expressing themselves as an organizing medium. The design of Christian education is a matter of deciding on sequences of activities and experiences by which the learning tasks may be effectively undertaken as goals and activities by individuals and groups.

Sequence is always governed fundamentally by the organizing principle. If that organizing principle is to be something in the nature of involvement in the life and work of the people of God, then three factors have to be taken into account in determining sequence:

163

The emergent tasks and activities of the worshiping, witnessing, working community, including its attention to the needs
of the world and the needs of developing persons.

The necessary information for intelligent, meaningful, and
effective participation in the life and work of the Christian
community.

The needs, capacities, and character of the developing and
maturing person coming into, within, and working out from
the Christian community.

The first would appear to imply quite specifically the learning task of listening (individually and corporately) with
growing alertness to the gospel and responding in faith and
love, as well as the learning task of assuming personal and
social responsibility in the light of the gospel.

The second implies the same learning task in so far as the
necessary information has to do with the gospel as the community's special message. Also implied are the learning tasks
of making contact, exploring, discovering, and appropriating
in the light of the gospel, since the necessary information
involves the whole scope of Christian education.

The third requires carefully worked out goals and activities
in terms of sequences and constellations. The need for the
most careful attention to this aspect is pointed to by Daniel A.
Prescott, in *The Child in the Educative Process,* where he has
provided reasons why the "traditional, piecemeal, lock-step
pattern of education" cannot work:

Children mature physically at strikingly different rates. But children constantly work on developmental tasks appropriate to their
organic-maturity levels; therefore, the motivation and needs of
children are determined by their organic maturity rather than by
their "mental ages." Mental ages and intelligence quotients are not
indices of maturity but of brightness, of learning capacity.

A child's perceptions—what experiences mean to him—are a function of his maturity level, cultural background, accumulated indi-

vidual experiences, values, goals, and emotional preoccupations. Children vary enormously in these, so a given classroom experience must have a different meaning for each child. Therefore, identical or standardized outcomes cannot be obtained from all children by the same instructional means.

Ideas and attitudes are not learned once and for all at a particular time. They grow and gain richer meaning as they are related to the experiences being accumulated by the child. Thus learning is a continuous process in every area of knowledge and not something that can be completed in a particular grade or through the study of a particular subject.

Each child's full and wholesome development requires that he work at many learning tasks not touched by the traditional curriculum. More than half his developmental tasks are not dealt with by these subjects, yet the accomplishment of these tasks is necessary to his development and therefore must become the concern of the school.

Difficult, emotion-producing adjustment problems occupy the attention of many children to the exclusion of most unrelated matters, such as the content of many subjects. Although they are not capable of much traditional subject-matter learning, they can profit tremendously from classroom experiences and interpersonal relationships at school, which contribute to meeting their emotional needs. And once they have made progress toward adjustment they often learn the necessary facts and skills with considerable rapidity. (Pp. 433–444.)

Further evidence of the requirement of attention to needs, capacities, and the character of the developing and maturing person is found in *A Look at Continuity in the School Program,* the Yearbook of the Association for Supervision and Curriculum Development, 1958:

Continuity of learning is what happens inside the individual learner as he has new experiences.

Continuity should be a matter of putting events, information, or situations into some kind of logical relationship with other events, information, or situations which have been a part of the experience of the individual. Since man is essentially a logical, reasoning being, it is proper to assume that this process of establishing continuity between present experience and past experiences is in constant operation throughout life.

Continuity is also a matter of selecting from an experience that course of action, information, or attitude which seems most logical in terms of one's self-interpreted needs, concerns, and desires. Man is a constant evaluator. Education's role in this activity should be that of improving the process by which children and youth select their learnings. Learners should have increasing understanding of their own developing needs and of the relationship of the needs to the means by which they can be met satisfactorily.

It is apparent that we cannot give continuity to children. Attempts to define scope and sequence in terms of graded subject matter or units to be covered have not achieved the best continuity of learning for all. It should be possible, however, to develop a teaching-learning situation wherein children and youth find it easier to gain a sense of wholeness and continuity in their learning.

To this end, the Yearbook considers three major conclusions:

Continuity requires knowledge and application of principles of child growth and development and principles of learning. (Chapter 7.)

Continuity is to be developed in terms of clear and specific immediate objectives that reflect the actual needs of the students, brought into focus by ultimate or general objectives. (Chapter 8.)

The logic of subject matter areas should be expressed in a way that will facilitate their mastery and at the same time serve the need for continuity of individual and group organization of experience. This calls for organization of the curriculum for continuity in terms of the basic understandings and concepts found in each of the subject matter fields which are essential to living in modern society (to replace outlines of specific knowledge and factual materials as objectives of teaching), and in terms of the skills needed to meet the continually recurring problems of living (developmental tasks). (Chapter 9.)

In the terminology that has been used in this discussion

so far, the second point above might be revised to read: "Continuity is to be developed in terms of clear and immediate specific objectives (group and individual goals that are specific aspects of the lifelong learning tasks) that reflect the actual needs of the students, brought into focus by ultimate or general objectives (the basic objective, scope, and themes, focused in the learning tasks)." The learning-tasks idea seems to go a step beyond the third proposal above. It fuses "concepts" and "skills" approaches into a more dynamic and unified process, while at the same time conserving all their values.

Sequence is thus directly related to the learning tasks, goals, and activities that the individual and the group undertake in Christian education. It tries to anticipate their changing needs and experiences in relation to God, man, the physical world, and history. In relation to their needs and experiences with various aspects of their world, sequence tends to be logical and systematic. This is really the matter of the scope of the curriculum (its logical continuity, horizontal continuity, horizontal articulation): the breadth of the learner's experience as the curriculum plans for it. In relation to their needs and experiences in their own growth and development, sequence tends to be psychological and developmental. This is the matter of sequence proper in the curriculum (its psychological continuity, vertical continuity, vertical articulation): the progression of the learner's experience as the curriculum plans for it.

The three factors may then be recognized as the principle having to be taken into account in the matter of sequence:

The principle of context: The life and work of the ongoing worshiping, witnessing, working community are crucial determinants of curriculum sequence.

The principle of scope: If we know the experiences to be included in the curriculum (the experiences related to God, man, the physical world, and history), we may proceed to use them in sequences in terms of the learning tasks.

The developmental principle: In developing content into sequences we seek to predict who the pupil is likely to be and what he is likely to need at various points and meet him there. This is worked out for individuals and groups on the basis of the factors involved in personality, motivation, learning, human growth and development, and group and sociocultural understandings. The curriculum should be pitched far enough ahead of the pupil to challenge him but not so far as to discourage.

This has implications for grouping and grading. If sequence is conceived in some such way as this and can be worked out on such a basis, the curriculum may be individualized and personalized. This means that individual experience, and group experience as well, may be enriched. Broadly graded groups may be handled in intelligently planned ways. This would seem to be true to the context of the witnessing community in its essential nature.

Prescott (pp. 436–439) reviews some promising adaptations of grouping and grading in the educative process. Among them are combination classes (classes of two mixed grades, with individual children working in groups within these classes), grade classification on the basis of chronological age, the "primary-unit" organization (units of three grades at a time, with individual children and groups progressing in their learnings at rates appropriate to their maturity levels, readiness, and capacities), and cutting across class lines (through such devices as student government and interclass committees).

A suggestion was made to the joint study committee that curriculum sequence be worked out through research on the learning tasks, as follows:

First, work out sequences involving developmental steps in listening and responding to the gospel.

Second, work out sequences of developmental steps in exploring the whole field of relationships (God, man, the physical world, history) in the light of the gospel, discovering meaning and value in the field of relationships in the light of the gospel, and appropriating that meaning and value personally.

Third, work out sequences involving developmental steps in assuming personal and social responsibility in the light of the gospel.

Fourth, integrate these sequences into patterns of sequences that would provide valid ways for persons to reach toward the objective of Christian education in unified comprehensively meaningful ways.

It was explained that this proposal would mean the anticipation of a variety of ways in which, in sequential steps, persons might reach toward the objective by undertaking the learning tasks as a lifelong matter. The fourth step in the proposal could not be done, it was felt, until the other three had been well worked out, but the curriculum would not really be ready for use until the fourth step had been completed.

When this proposal was made there was little forewarning of the difficulties that would arise in trying to work it out. Two years of experience with it have shown some of the misunderstandings about the whole process that have had to be corrected, particularly in the understanding of the way in which the task of "listening and responding" relates to the other four tasks.

A further note on sequence, appropriate at this point, is found in the senior high document (pp. 36–37): The learning tasks are interrelated in one dynamic process. They do not necessarily occur in the order in which they are listed. Their general sequence is in this order, but they are used and repeated in varying order in reaching the objective. Thus the object of learning must not be assumed to have been achieved simply because the various learning tasks have been undertaken. This is why their repetition is often necessary. Any discovery of meaning and value raises new questions, presents new problems, and opens up new vistas for exploration. Any personal appropriation of meaning and value requires further exploration and the probing of meaning and value in the resultant experience. The viewing of meaning and value in the light of the gospel inevitably involves reconsideration of all experience and the undertaking of new duties. The assumption of responsibility may initiate learning, accompany it, or result from it.

One of the educational needs to be considered is, as DeWolf puts it, "the need for order, the need for the learner to see a systematic and planned sequence within which he is making progress. An authoritative course through which one must work has positive values. Also, the group's need for community requires order." In view of this need, there is undoubtedly a place in curriculum-building for the kind of orderly sequential approach suggested by the following steps that might be taken in framing certain aspects of curriculum:

Step 1: Categorize in an inclusive and detailed way the things to be experienced, understood, and achieved.

Step 2: Analyze the steps and methods involved in connection with each of these.

Step 3: Estimate where in the development of the individual each of the steps and methods is likely to fall. (At each developmental level there is a possibility of response of faith and life as against a response of faithlessness, rejection, and death.)

Step 4: Estimate the variations involved in developmental anticipation of each of the steps and methods.

Step 5: Work out developmental clusters of experiences, understandings, and achievements.

Step 6: Refine and relate them so that there is some idea of possible integrated and inclusive progression for each age level, with variations.

Step 7: Establish major and minor governing motifs for the various developmental levels, with variations.

Attention to sequence, as might be predicted, often creates difficulties in attention to scope. Dealing with the whole scope at once is unmanageable; yet, dealing with a segment of it leads to a sense of fragmentation and of having missed the point. Furthermore, it is very easy to become confused about the relation of the gospel to the entire scope of Christian education, so that the meaning of undertaking the learning tasks in the light of the gospel becomes unclear.

But the fact is that in life persons are constantly occupied with exploring, discovering meaning and value, and appropriating meaning and value in the field of relationships—in home, school, and life in general. This is going on all the time anyway in some form, and curriculum planners are by no means solely responsible for it. Persons are taking trips, earning money, talking, reading, listening, deciding; the curriculum cannot be as real to them as some of these other activities unless it adjusts its sequence to take account of them and use them. In determining sequence, it is the part of wisdom to use what is being learned in school. Furthermore, sequence must be adjusted in view of the multiple contacts that the church has with the pupil in various groups, choirs, clubs, home, and the rest.

The task of the curriculum planner in Christian education is not to plan all of educational experience but to focus upon the experience of the gospel and its communication, helping the person to focus the rest of his experience meaningfully in the gospel. In the process, the curriculum planner will also try to see that the field of relationships is understood, grasped, and used as weighed, related, and developed in the scope of Christian education. It is just as important to communicate the way in which the field of relationships becomes the scope of Christian education as it is to communicate its substance.

This is what the objective of Christian education and the scope of Christian education seem clearly to imply. Furthermore, the learning-tasks idea keeps that scope in focus. Other approaches tend to let it remain fragmentary. This does not mean, however, that in the learning-tasks approach specifics are not dealt with. Far from it. The specifics are embodied in group and individual goals, aspects of the learning tasks. The lifelong tasks, however, are clearly focused upon the whole field of relationships in the light of the gospel. Therefore, every group or individual goal, however specific, is to be clearly related to the scope.

We may assume that, in the main, in the ordinary course of the person's experience, exploration, discovery, and personal appropriation of meaning and value are taking place on the basis of the assumption of personal and social responsibility. But we may not assume that they are taking place in terms of the scope of Christian education or in the light of the gospel.

Thus, primary attention to "listening with growing alertness to the gospel and responding in faith and love" is called for, together with training in how to carry on the other learning tasks in the light of experience in listening and responding to the gospel. This appears to shed new and needed light on the way in which the proposal for the development of sequence might be implemented.

Listening . . . responding . . . If the scope of Christian education has been analyzed correctly, the essentials in "listening and responding" are to be found in the Bible and the life of the church. This is so because the Bible and the life of the church are the means through which the Word is made known to us, the Word in turn being the way in which God—Father, Son, and Holy Spirit—has chosen to come to man. Furthermore, it is in the Bible and the life of the church that we find ourselves called into relationship with God and through which he throws the light we need on the rest of the field of relationships—man, nature, and history—so that we may see them in the new perspective of the gospel.

Rachel Henderlite made this point at one of the joint study sessions when she put the principle in this way:

We have one central job, to listen with growing alertness to the message, which is that we are members of the household of God. Then we go out from the place where we are gathered together as members of the household of God and dare to face whatever we have to face in the light of the basic conviction that "I now belong to God and to this community entrusted by God to live here in this way."

Several years ago I sat down beside a teacher who gave voice lessons in New York City. In the course of the conversation he said that he usually taught a half-hour lesson (I thought, Sunday school does too) and charged five dollars (this was some time ago) for one of these lessons. I asked him what in the world you could teach a person in half an hour that would be worth five dollars! He said, and I think this is our clue, "I don't have to sit by this person while he sees all of the implications of everything I tell him, while he practices and drills, and comes to understand its meaning. All I need to do is to give him a basic insight into what to do with his voice, then he goes out and does it for himself."

Essentially we are to convey, nonverbally as well as verbally, the great central fact that we belong to the community of the people of God, the household of faith that God has brought into being through the acts testified to through the Bible story and accomplished through his work in the world today.

If the essentials of "listening with growing alertness to the gospel and responding in faith and love" are to be found in the Bible and the life of the church, a position that is in accord with the organizing principle, this learning task may be analyzed in terms of the kinds of functions that define the life and work of the Christian community:

Involvement in the worshiping, witnessing, working community's study:
    of the Bible,
    of doctrine,

of the history of the church and its encounter with the
world,

of contemporary affairs, as the present scene of God's
working.

Involvement in the community's worship.

Involvement in the community's creative expression of its
faith and life:

through music,

through the spoken word,

through literature,

through the other arts.

Involvement in the community's witness.

Involvement in the community's service.

Involvement in the community's social action.

Involvement in the fellowship of the common life.

Involvement in the extension of the community's fellowship
through the outreach of mission.

Involvement in the community's practice of stewardship, including vocation.

In the analysis of this learning task in the senior high
document, the first set of activities involved are:

Taking part in the worship, life, and work of the church.

Studying the Bible in order to know the gospel.

Praying.

The first two of these clusters of activities are directly stated
above in the list of the kinds of functions that define the life
and work of the community of faith. The whole list might
well be considered to be an attempt at brief but comprehensive
expansion of these two clusters of activities.

The third activity, praying, recalls to us the essential fact
that every involvement stated above has its personal and individual side, as well as its corporate side. Prayer, for instance,
is an essential personal aspect of worship.

Further, what is meant by involvement is the personal par-

ticipation of free persons—involvement in community that
frees and personalizes, not involvement in a collective that en-
slaves, narrows one's outlook, or depersonalizes (as Erich
Kahler puts it in *The Tower and the Abyss*).

To take the implications of the personal side of this involvement another step—the transformation of the person, his conversion—is inescapable. Thus the analysis of this learning task
in the document includes, as a second set of activities:

> Repenting in the light of the gospel.
> Accepting the gospel.
> Receiving the gospel.
> Depending upon the gospel.

The sequence of the other tasks is applicable to the task of
"listening and responding." Involvement in the church's life
and work means exploration of this crucial aspect of the field
of relationships, discovery of meaning and value in it, personal
appropriation of that meaning and value, and the assumption
of personal and social responsibility throughout. The "spiraling cycles of exploration, discovery, and appropriation, undergirded by the assumption of responsibility," apply as well to
the Bible and the life of the church as to any other aspects of
experience.

Each aspect of involvement in the life and work of the
Christian community may be expressed as goal and activity
(for instance, "studying doctrine and participating in the
process of theologizing—creating contemporaneously relevant
doctrine through reflecting on the human situation in the light
of God's revealed Word"); each such goal and activity may be
subjected to sequential analysis in terms of the sequence of
human development and the sequence of developing events in
the life and concerns of the church, and thus sequences of
goals and activities useful for curriculum purposes produced,
subordinate to the learning task of listening with growing
alertness to the gospel and responding in faith and love.

Throughout one's undertaking of the learning tasks in the

context of the life and work of the church there is a basic sequence of perceiving the gospel, accepting the gospel, and discovering and fulfilling the gospel's demands. While it is undeniable that all three of these are essential factors at every developmental stage, it is probably true that in childhood the major motif is perception of the gospel; in adolescence, acceptance of the gospel; and in adulthood, discovering and fufilling the demands of the gospel. This may well be the clue to the developmental side of sequence in Christian education.

Another essential factor was highlighted by L. Harold DeWolf in his presentation on scope and sequence before the joint study committee:

> *We ought to teach the whole range of the scope at all age levels, though assuredly the manner, detail, and depth of the instruction will vary greatly.*
>
> Having taught, in recent years, in church school kindergarten, adult class, and senior department, I should say that the kindergarten made as great demands on my theology, as well as on my faith, as have the adult class or the teen-agers.
>
> The longer I have taught at both senior and adult levels, the more firmly convinced I am that the *whole* gospel must be taught at each of these levels, almost as if it had never been taught before. So new is the emotional, volitional, and ideational context at each of these levels that the gospel itself is likely to appear now as a great mystery and even novelty.

Bringing the gospel to bear upon the rest of life's meaning and value. In what ways are exploration of the field of relationships, discovery of meaning and value, personal appropriation of that meaning and value, and assumption of personal and social responsibility taking place in the rest of life? Real guidance is found here in Havighurst's analysis of developmental tasks and education in *Human Development and Education,* and in the anlysis of persistent life situations and the ways in which learners face them that has been made by the Horace Mann-Lincoln School Institute of School Experimentation and included in Stratemeyer (and others), *Developing a Curriculum for Modern Living* (especially pp. 146–332), and in the listing of activities associated with each of the learning tasks in the senior high document.

But the further question for Christian education is that of bringing the gospel to bear upon the rest of life's meaning and value. The most thorough treatment of this matter is to be found in the Lutheran document, *The Functional Objectives for Christian Education*, Vol. I. The last two paragraphs of the analysis of the first learning task in the senior high document also provide a clue:

> Growing in realization of the implications and demands of the gospel, particularly as they relate to (the rest of the field of relationships).
>
> Reviewing, re-examining, and reconstructing discoveries and personal appropriations of meaning and value in the light of the gospel.

The sequence of Christian education curriculum will thus inevitably be "sequences" if the problem is faced realistically. There will be sequences for individuals, generally related to the sequences of experiences that learning groups are undertaking. As individuals and groups undertake the learning tasks of Christian education, careful and thorough planning is to be done on group and individual goals. As these are planned (in the light of the way in which individuals and groups may deal with the whole field of relationships in the light of the gospel) sequences will emerge. As they are carried through, sequences will be realized.

FLEXIBILITY

Flexibility in the curriculum means that it should be changeable and adaptable in terms of the educational settings where it is to be used, in terms of method, and in terms of individual, community, and cultural differences. Such flexibility is essential if the curriculum is to have immediate meaning and relevance to the persons and groups engaged as learners, teachers, and leaders in Christian education. Differences are to be expected and planned for. In a sense these differences must be considered the rule and not exceptional.

Individual differences. What do we need to know about the abilities, interests, and needs of the learner? How may we find out? How may this help us to clarify and set goals?

The child study movement has for many years had a profound influence upon education in emphasizing that we need to know pupils personally in order to be able to guide them through helping them to develop and achieve their own goals in the light of readiness and other factors. Recently, special concern for the handicapped and the gifted has been growing.

Major aids in individualization of the curriculum are the many means at the teacher's disposal for getting to know the learner: observation, anecdotal records, autobiographies, testing, sociometry (the study of the popular and rejected members of the class by which cliques and isolates are found), rating scales (used as a basis for discussing with the pupil his opinion of his abilities and achievement). The chief aid is still the personal conference, in which the teacher simply talks with the person in a mood of acceptance, understanding, and communication. This is not to be confused with counseling, which has different purposes and which requires additional training.

One church, in its nursery school, maintains records on individual children, covering physical development, language development, response to routines, response to materials, response to children, response to adults, emotional development, and cumulative teacher evaluations of growth.

The use of records, reports, and case studies may be built into curriculum plans in order to foster individualization. So may co-operative planning of individual and group goals in the classroom, co-operative planning being the clue to preserving and using the values of group experience in taking individual differences into account.

Community differences. In Effie G. Bathurst's *Where Chil-*

dren Live Affects Curriculum it is pointed out that "the curricular activities in which children engage in solving real-life problems are often different in different regions, communities, and neighborhoods where the children live. Among the influences on curricular activities are geography and natural resource, industry, history, ancestry and culture, wealth or income level, social status, race, and communities' attitudes and folkways. Some of the influences are characteristic of large regions. Others are simple ways of living that may be found in one city or county and not in another" (p. iv).

The curriculum may take the factor of community differences into account by including means for analyzing the characteristics and needs of the community; means for determining the influence of the community on the church, the family, the teacher, and the pupil; and means for finding and using community resources. Among the guideposts listed in Bathurst's pamphlet for curriculum-building in community life are: resources and problems in the environment (the basic culture, the mingling of cultures, differences in economic re sources); assistance from parents in developing and carrying out the curriculum as it relates to community factors; the climate; arts and handicrafts in the community; local industries; and local historical materials.

Cultural differences. Many cultural differences show up as community differences. Yet there are factors, such as language and vocabulary, that often have more far-reaching roots than the local community.

Words mean different things to different people, because of the cultural background that they bring to them. Furthermore, the vocabulary of the individual may be limited or extensive depending upon the cultural rootage in which it is founded. A sound curriculum will take account of these differences as they show up in the group and give ample opportunity for the kind of give-and-take and common experiences that will enable understanding to grow and to be expressed in common language. This is especially important when cultural differences are accompanied by great differences of religious background.

In face of difficulties in communication, which are character-istic of every classroom whether cultural differences are marked or not, the curriculum should give the most serious attention to those creative activities which are nonverbal in nature (music, art, and the like) and should be especially rich in audio-visual materials through which a multisensory impres-sion may overcome language and vocabulary problems more rapidly than otherwise.

At the same time "cultural constellations of experience" found in the group may be an invaluable curriculum resource, providing a basis for intercultural experiences in the planning and carrying out of group and individual goals.

Remedial work. The question of various kinds of differences and their curriculum implications raises the question of re-medial work. In approaching remedial work in Christian edu-cation it is necessary to keep in mind that not every one in the grade, class, or group is supposed to be at the same level of achievement. The matter is complicated by the fact that the individual's responses tend to be unitary, which would lead the teacher to judge that he is "ahead of," "with," or "behind" his group or age level in achievement. The curriculum can help the teacher to avoid unitary judgments, helping him to see that when he looks at the whole gamut of the learner's responses, marked maturity may show up in certain areas, while marked immaturity may show up in others. One of the dangers of uni-tary judgments is that they tend to stick when they are no longer true.

The curriculum may give hints on what to do with regard to classroom climate, home relations, relations with school and other groups, and possibilities of referrals. It can show how to find out in what ways the learner is immature and in what ways he is mature; how to capitalize on his areas of maturity in skills, attitudes, and behavior; how to use leadership re-sponsibilities and projects in manual areas. The curriculum can show how to motivate the learner to work on his deficiencies and accelerate his progress, not putting everything else aside, however, to work on his deficiencies.

Educational settings. Part of the curriculum problem is to devise an adequate setting or settings in which Christian education may take place. This is always in process. It begins with the vision of the church as the setting, that is, the fellowship of Christian believers, together with their children, living the Christian life and doing their work. It takes particular forms, however, as the church becomes conscious of itself and analytical with regard to the modes of educating into its life and work. Thus various institutional settings for Christian education come into being.

Since it is in process, the church has at any given time various institutional settings in terms of which it does its educational work. It inherits them; it invents them; it borrows them from the secular community; it shares them with the secular community; it eliminates some from time to time; it remodels some from time to time; it makes new combinations from time to time.

The curriculum is, of course, prepared primarily to be used in specific educational settings. While in the process of thinking through the implications of curriculum theory, new ideas for educational settings are bound to occur to us.

The following list includes some settings that are exclusively the church's; in some it co-operates; some are independent but in their own way do things that have implications for the religious nurture of the child, youth, or adult. They indicate the range of the curriculum's flexibility of design, so far as its educational setting is concerned.

Adult schools
Assemblies (national and regional)
Bible-study groups
Camps
Canteens
Caravans
Career conferences
Children's homes
Choirs
Church boards
Church family nights
Clinics (teachers and leaders)
Clubs

Coaching conferences (previews)
Colleges and universities
Committees
Communicants classes
Conferences
Congregational worship
Conventions
Co-operative play groups
Correspondence schools
Couples clubs
Craft groups
Day camps
Demonstration schools
Evangelistic programs
Family camps
Family services
Fellowship cells (small groups)
Group work agencies
Home
Homes for the aged
Hospitals
Hostels
House churches
Independent schools
Industrial missions
Institutes
Junior church
Laboratory schools
Leadership training schools
Men's associations
Ministers in industry
Mission schools
Missionary groups
Monastic communities
Nursery schools
Parents' groups
Parish conferences
Prayer schools

Prisons
Public schools
Radio
Recreation groups
Reformatories
Resident camps
Resident communities
Retreats
School camps
Schools for living
Seminaries
Settlement houses
Skill shops
Special schools
Student foundations
Study centers
Study tours
Summer camps
Summer service groups
Sunday afternoon groups
Sunday church school
 —closely graded
 —departmentally graded
 —ungraded
Sunday evening groups
Television
Theaters
University of life
Vacation church schools
Wednesday summer church
  school
Weekday church schools
Women's associations
Work camps
Young adult conferences
Youth centers
Youth conferences

Methods. What is a particular method good for? The curriculum should provide sound guidance on the selection and use of the most appropriate methodology in the light of the principles that have been developed to govern the educational process. The teacher should be given guidance on how to select the method most appropriate to the given situation he and his group are facing.

To this end, standard analyses of method for Christian education need to be developed, by which it may be shown what is involved in any particular method and by which its suitability may be determined. Such standard analyses would include for any proposed method:

Its history.
A description of what it is and what it involves.
The materials needed to use it.
Steps in preparing to use it.
Steps in using it.
Steps in follow-up
Time required for its use.
Its theological, functional, and developmental uses and limitations.
Variations of the method.
Related methods (that properly precede, complement, or follow the use of this method).

There should be built into the curriculum definite suggestions on how to use such analyses in arriving at methodological decisions.

Setting and method themselves should be required to vary according to individual, community, and cultural differences. One of the chief challenges to Christian education at the present time is to free itself from any stereotype as to setting or method and approach the redesigning of curriculum with the utmost imagination and individuality. Any setting is to be designed and evaluated in terms of its conduciveness to the achievement of the objective. Any method that implements the objective effectively is to be considered seriously for use. Thus setting and method are to be allowed to vary quite freely according to differences in need, background, and ability (individual, community, and cultural).

The key to flexibility is in setting and planning to achieve individual and group goals. These goals may vary as widely as various settings, methods, and differences require, providing they are always clearly related to one or more of the Christian learning tasks. If the pertinent goals clearly involve undertaking some important aspect of the Christian learning tasks, the curriculum cannot be considered to be off base. Flexibility is thus possible because of the definiteness of the context, purpose, scope, and process of Christian education. Flexibility is facilitated by the fact that the learning tasks provide an organizing medium that is at one and the same time stable and free.

Chapter 7

DEVELOPING CURRICULUM MATERIALS

C URRICULUM MATERIALS consist of suggestions and resources to be used to guide, inform, and enrich the teaching-learning process as individuals and groups undertake that process. A review of what is basically involved will indicate the setting for the use of these materials.

In the teaching-learning situation we set and work at group and individual goals. How are these goals arrived at? From one side, they are the product of learners' personal ends, leaders' personal ends, and group ends, combined with the church's purpose, using the basic objective of Christian education as the guide. Needs, experiences, and situation (past, present, and future) figure in setting the specific goals that we work on and the activities through which those goals will be sought.

From the other side, these group and individual goals are specific aspects of the Christian learning tasks, involving topics and problems drawn from and related to the scope of Christian education, in order to accomplish the basic objective.

When we have sufficiently worked on these particular group and individual goals in the teaching-learning process we take our bearings, in terms of behavioral outcomes, new personal ends, the total scope of our task, and the basic objective. We

then decide on next steps in developmental sequence and set
and work at new group and individual goals.

Such a process has tremendous breadth, pointedness, life,
and dynamic, involving as it does the whole field of relationships, the Christian church and gospel, and the powerful personal ends of the individual and the group. To make the
suggestions and provide key resources that will put each of
these at the service of the others is the task of curriculum
materials.

CURRICULUM MATERIALS

Considerations of sequence and flexibility require the use
of such materials as the curriculum guide, area guides, resource units, and teaching-learning units. *The curriculum
guide* is a basic manual that explains what a curriculum of
Christian education is, the ingredients that make it up, and
how it may be built and used. *Area guides* are collections
of goals, content, activities, and materials of instruction, showing how each of the major curricular areas may be handled
through the life span. *Resource units* are also collections of
goals, content, activities, and materials of instruction but deal
with more segmented topics or problems, usually at one level
(children, youth, or adults), although certain topics and problems may lend themselves to ungraded resource units. *Teaching-learning units* are for the use of teachers and learners in
the local church and provide specific plans and suggestions.

The curriculum guide. The curriculum guide will be a substantial volume dealing with the fundamentals of curriculum
planning, to be used on the interdenominational, denominational, regional, community, and local parish levels. If it were
prepared interdenominationally, denominational supplements would be useful in providing the particular additional
information that a communion would want to see in the
picture for its parishes and groups as they work at curriculum.

The contents of a curriculum guide will cover the following
concerns:

1. The basic principles of curriculum:
     a. The context of Christian education.
     b. The scope of Christian education.
     c. The purpose of Christian education.
     d. The process of Christian education.
     e. The organizing principle of the curriculum.
2. An exposition of the learning tasks in Christian education:
     a. The tasks themselves: what they are and what they mean.
     b. Their implementation of the basic principles.
     c. The educational and learning theory upon which they are based.
     d. Their use in curriculum.
3. An analysis of curricular areas (guides, based on the scope, to the derivation of topics and problems; themes):
     a. The curricular areas themselves:
          The Word of God.
          The theological task.
          What the church is and does.
          The church in history.
          The church in today's world.
          Human relations.
          The realization of the self.
          The Christian life.
     b. How these curricular areas might be used and developed as area guides and resource units and how they would lend themselves in that connection to interpretation in terms of specific group and individual goals.
4. A discussion of the learner (the learning group and the individual):
     a. Suggestions on how to study the individual student, indicating specific techniques to use, the types of records to keep, and how to use the findings in making curriculum decisions.

   b. Suggestions on how to study the group as a group.
   c. A statement of the kinds of characteristics, needs, and
      developmental tasks that are likely to be encount-
      ered.
5. A discussion of how to proceed in the teaching-learning
situation with a group and with individuals:
   a. An outline of the process itself.
   b. Suggestions on how to plan co-operatively with the
      group.
   c. Techniques for developing topics and problems and
      group and individual goals out of the ongoing situ-
      ation of the student, his life, and his group work.
6. An analysis of basic learning experiences, in terms of
methods and activities (using the standard methodological
analyses suggested in Chapter 6).
7. An analysis and evaluation of basic types of resource
materials.
8. A comprehensive analysis of possibilities of over-all sequence in terms of steps in developmental sequence.
9. A discussion of how to evaluate program, process, and
group and individual achievement.
10. A discussion of how to analyze a particular parish and
set up its curriculum:
   a. Community and parish analysis of situation, need,
      and resources (including "personalization" of the
      mission of the church and the objective of Chris-
      tian education in this particular parish).
   b. How to select and use (or develop) teaching-learning
      units in this particular parish.
   c. How to provide for periodic review and redirection
      of the curriculum of the parish.
   d. How to provide adequate access to personal super-
      visory help in planning and evaluating locally.

If such contents as suggested above were used, one basic
curriculum guide for Protestant education, plus denomina-

tional supplements (both periodically revised), would be sufficient.

Area guides. An area guide is a rich reservoir of ideas and possibilities, dealing with one of the major areas of curriculum, from which may be drawn the more specific ideas and possibilities in the resource unit (from which, in turn, teaching-learning units may be drawn). Thus at least several resource units may be expected to spring from a single area guide.

An area guide offers a comprehensive and varied list of suggestions, activities, and materials on one of the curriculum's chief topical concerns, covering the treatment of this topic and its correlated problems throughout the learner's life span. Working out area guides is the first step in getting the principles of the curriculum guide into shape for the development of curriculum. The sum of the area guides (there should be only as many as there are *major* curriculum areas) provides the comprehensive picture of the whole curriculum.

Such a wide variety of possibilities as is included in an area guide makes it possible for the curriculum builder to provide for flexibility in the more specific resource units and in the even more specific teaching-learning units. This, in the end, makes it possible for the teacher to bring the learner into the planning process.

An area guide will cover Christian education concerns for its particular topic in a variety of settings. The Sunday church school, the vacation church school, the weekday church school, Sunday evening groups, the women's association, the men's association, and all the rest, will be borne clearly in mind. The test of a good area guide (as of a good resource unit) is the flexibility with which it handles its topic in terms of the requirements of such a variety of situations.

What makes up an area guide? The following outline of contents may be used in designing an area guide for Christian education:

1. The topic.
2. Motivations and personal ends related to the topic:
    a. An analysis of understandings and misunderstandings, questions, and felt needs that may be expected to exist in the area covered by the topic.
    b. Clues to help identify unfelt needs and engender other motivations.
3. The intent of the topic in relation to the objective of Christian education.
4. The scope of the topic:
    a. The portion of the scope of Christian education covered by the topic.
    b. The relation of the topic to the total scope of Christian education.
    c. The relation of the topic to the scope of other area guides and resource units.
5. Group and individual goals:
    a. An explanation of how to arrive at group and individual goals.
    b. A statement of such goals in connection with this topic and its correlated problems in the form of a possible range or sequence of goals:
        A range of introductory goals or activities.
        A range of developmental goals or activities.
        A range of culminating goals or activities.
    c. Standard analyses of the goals that are of central importance:
        The name or other definitive designation of the goal or activity being analyzed. (Goals and activities may be stated with varying degrees of specificity. For instance, "learning about history," almost completely lacks specificity. "Identifying major events and problems of the Reformation" is much more specific. "Designing and making a time line of the book of The Acts" is so concrete that one may visualize the actual procedures in-

volved. The listing and analyzing of the goals and activities should probably proceed from the five general learning tasks to the more specific ones, with the relations between them clearly indicated.)

Description:

What is the point of the goal of activity?

What procedures are involved in carrying it out?

What materials are utilized?

What persons are ordinarily involved?

What kinds of outcomes may ordinarily be expected?

Which of the five general learning tasks is it related to? In what ways?

What aspects of the scope of Christian education are involved? How?

Is it related to any one or more age or experience levels in particular?

What goals or activities necessarily precede or lead up to this one?

What goals or activities appropriately follow from this one?

6. Detailed description of possible procedures. These will consist of various methods, activities, and projects. Drawing upon the materials above, broadening and exploratory experiences should be suggested for the beginning of the work and integrating experiences for the end, in accordance with the progressive nature of the learning tasks. Methods will usually be described in detail. It is useful to show several possible lines of development, especially for groups of any size, which will follow directly from the range of suggested group and individual goals (one for slow learners, emphasizing physically active and creative expressional ways of learning; one for average learners; and one for fast learners, emphasizing mental achievement and research, integrating other activities with them). It should be shown in some detail how these lines of

development may be used at the same time, contributing to one another's achievement of the group goals. Part of the plan development is to show how motivations may be developed, how they may be sustained, and what to do if they do not develop.

7. Resources, lists of materials, and bibliographies. This will contain study materials and other aids. These should be broken down into functional categories, that is, in terms of the service they are supposed to perform.

8. Procedures for evaluation:
   a. An approach to continuous evaluation.
   b. An approach to objective evaluation, weighing values, weighing content and procedures, and examining individual and group work.
   c. Rechecking progress and achievement and considering implications for next steps.

Area guides are to be built covering curricular areas in terms of wide age spans. The suggestions developed so far in this book would indicate something like the following eight areas for area guides: the Word of God, the theological task, what the church is and does, the church in history, the church in today's world, human relations, the realization of the self, and the Christian life.

By their very nature, area guides are most valuable when developed in substantial, semipermanent form. They need, of course, to be subject to periodic revision.

Resource units. A resource unit is a rich reservoir of ideas and possibilities, as is an area guide. But a resource unit is more limited in scope than is an area guide, and is usually, although not always, designed with a particular age level (children, youth, or adults) in mind. Thus, while an area guide is built on a topic like "The Church in History," resource units in the same area would deal with such topics as "Apostolic Times," "The Reformation," "The History of Methodism," or "The Church in America." Furthermore, each of these might be aimed at one particular age level.

There are exceptions to the age-level rule on resource units. When a topic lends itself to better treatment across age levels than on one particular level, it should be developed in that way. For instance, a resource unit on "Stewardship," or one on "Christian Responsibility in Our Community," could be developed best across age levels, but they would still be resource units rather than area guides because of the nature of the topics with which they dealt.

Perhaps the major function of the area guides is to fill in the outline of the curriculum so that it may be seen whole, while the major function of the resource unit is to provide the curriculum builder with the material he needs for the construction of teaching-learning units. Its flexibility is consciously built in, as is that of the area guide, and is passed on to the teaching-learning units that it informs.

A resource unit may be built to serve a variety of educational settings. The variety will usually not be so wide as that of the area guide. Nevertheless, at the children's level a resource unit will provide the guidance needed for curriculum construction in the Sunday church school, the vacation church school, the weekday church school, the home, clubs, and the rest. At the youth level, it will provide the guidance needed for Sunday morning and evening groups, for the home, for weekday groups, for the individual's study, and possibly even for camp and conference curriculum. At the adult level it will serve to guide the study program, men's and women's organizations, the home, parents' groups, and similar situations.

What makes up a resource unit? The same outline as that of the area guide is to be used for the resource unit, with the understanding that the topic is more limited and that, with exceptions, the unit is designed for a particular age level.

Resource units, being of more limited scope yet more numerous than area guides, are most valuable when produced in pamphlet or booklet form. In this form they are permanent enough to be given serious and steady use, yet may be readily revised and brought up to date. In this form also, new resource units may be introduced when needed, and obsolete units withdrawn, without upsetting the balance and structure of the curriculum.

Teaching-learning units. Teaching-learning units offer specific ideas for group use. They are guides for particular groups for particular times, drawn from resource units. While the resource unit is more particularly for the use of the curriculum builder, the teaching-learning unit is intended particularly for the teacher and learner in the local church.

Teaching-learning units are of two kinds. One type of teaching-learning unit provides specific session plans, "prepackaged" for the teacher and learner. These "prepackaged" units are often referred to in public education as "teaching units." Even such units may allow for involving teachers and learners in joint planning at many points.

The other type of teaching-learning unit is a more flexible resource, inviting the teaching-learning group to proceed on something of a "do it yourself" basis and providing the necessary guidance and ingredients for them.

The basic design of the curriculum is outlined in the curriculum guide, spelled out in area guides, and put in specific shape for flexible and detailed curriculum development in resource units. Using the resource units, a denomination or group of denominations may choose to issue either or both types of teaching-learning units for use in its churches. The decision as to the type of teaching-learning unit to be offered undoubtedly depends upon two factors: which type of unit best suits the content to be dealt with, and the degree to which leaders are trained and able to handle the more flexible approach to teaching and learning.

The teaching-learning unit is specific as to the scope of its content and as to the scope of the experience it projects for the teaching-learning situation. It offers a limited number of suggestions, which can be selected and used according to the teachers' or learners' judgment of the needs and interests of the group in its situation. The teaching-learning unit and its supporting pupil text or reading materials offer content aimed specifically at the students for their use session by session.

A single teaching-learning unit may conceivably serve its purpose in a number of different settings: Sunday church school, vacation church school, weekday church school, camp, conference, and the like.

The content of a teaching-learning unit involves items such as the following:

1. The topic or problem.
2. The rationale for the topic or problem, in terms of the significance of its content and the needs it seeks to meet.
3. The goals that are sought (a range of goals, selected to represent the variety of backgrounds, abilities, needs, and interests likely to be found in the group).
4. The content and experiences to be included.
5. Resources (books and other materials) to be used.
6. A plan for introducing the study and getting the pupils interested in it.
7. Either specific session plans, or suggestions for developing session plans, covering:
    a. Exploratory discussions and activities.
    b. Co-operative planning.
    c. Gathering information.
    d. Organizing the ideas gathered.
    e. Checking on understanding.
    f. Summarizing.
8. A plan for evaluation:
    a. Growth and changes in the group.
    b. Individual strengths, weaknesses, problems.

In terms of local church use, denominations might develop the more flexible type of teaching-learning unit and place it in the hands of teachers and leaders in the local parish, so that they and the learners, with adequate supervisory help, might develop their own teaching-learning plans. On the other hand, denominations might develop preplanned teaching-learning units for leaders in the local parish; this would be similar to the procedure now followed by the majority of churches, except that the product would be related to a common series of resource units.

Guidance manuals. Although the curriculum guide and the resource units would contain full explanations of their use in shaping up parish curriculums and group teaching-learning programs, it might be desirable to select out of these guides and units those materials particularly needed by the parish on the one hand, and the teacher or leader of a group on the other, and incorporate them in a guide for churches in shaping its curriculum and a guide for teachers and leaders on developing teaching-learning units from resource units.

Such manuals would be most useful if they contained not just the basic principles but illustrative case material drawn from the experience of churches in curriculum planning.

Resource materials. What other supporting material will be needed by churches, groups, and individuals? Here the richest variety of materials should be produced and made available for use in connection with the resource units. Among the categories of materials needed are:

Textbooks.
Books for collateral reading.
Family resource books.
Materials for individual study.
Guides to individual and group action.
Nonprojected visual materials (maps, pictures, posters, etc.).
Projected audio-visual materials (films, filmstrips, etc.).
Books on teaching-learning.

All aspects of the scope of Christian education and all the involvements of the church's life and work should be taken into account in setting up and producing these materials.

EVALUATION IN CURRICULUM

All the various aspects of the curriculum enterprise need evaluation from time to time. The basic conception or theory of curriculum needs constant scrutiny. The process of teaching and learning as it is actually carried out, and in which the curriculum comes to life, needs periodic examination. The processes of designing and producing curriculum materials need evaluation. The materials themselves require attentive analysis and criticism. The outcomes achieved in the lives of the participants and members need to be looked at.

The evaluation guides, the specific criteria used for judging, and the procedures for evaluation will be different for each of these aspects as it is being examined. The fundamental test in each case, however, is this, "In what ways has this aspect of the curriculum process contributed, or failed to contribute, to the achievement of the basic purpose of Christian education?" In the case of personal and group outcomes the appropriate form of the question is, "What evidences are there of awareness of the gospel and response in faith and love?"

The criteria for evaluation of any aspect of the curriculum enterprise ought not to stray far from the basic purpose of Christian education and the concepts of context, scope, and process that are so closely related to it. Objectives and anticipated outcomes that are too specific are presumptuous and tend to make rigid that which should remain fluid, to tie down that which should be free, to reflect moralism rather than the life of grace, and to substitute human judgment for the will of God. Furthermore, attention to detailed goals can be seriously misleading in the fragmentariness with which they relate to the objective of Christian education; it is better to use outcomes factually as descriptions to be checked against the objective than to set them up conceptually as criteria by which to judge the adequacy of results.

In other words, we are in a good position at the present time in Christian education to proceed with evaluation of plans, materials, structure, and process. To do so, we need to seek evidence of the presence and appropriate use of the basic principles and processes that we have formulated and discovered (context, scope, purpose, process, organizing principle, and learning tasks). Generally, the factors in evaluation of any aspect of the curriculum process will include:

Delineation of the aspect of curriculum to be evaluated (process, personal outcomes, materials, etc.).

Gathering of pertinent facts and analysis of the situation.

Setting of criteria by which to render evaluative judgment.

Systematic examination of the situation in the light of the criteria.

Framing of evaluative judgments.

Communication of judgments to the proper persons and groups for their consideration and action.

The evaluation of the institutions that seek to promote Christian growth is best done with the use of surveys and institutional case studies. These include information on purposes, setting, relationships (internal, and to the community and others), organization, program, personnel, participation, management, building and equipment, finance, etc. Evaluation is often in the form of self-study by a regularly constituted committee or by one especially appointed for this purpose. Sometimes expert help from the outside (denominational field people or university research groups) is required.

The evaluation of program and curriculum (including the teaching-learning process) involves survey and theoretical analysis, with periodic scrutiny of basic purposes, the interests and needs of participants, standards, and available resources. It also requires live supervision, teacher-observer teams, group self-supervision using group dynamics techniques, group self-study, and the like. This may be done at any level of program and curriculum for a total parish, or even for a denomination. "Action research," described by Hilda Taba and Elizabeth Noel in *Action Research: A Case Study,* is a technique by which leaders and participants may use a problem-solving method in on-the-spot research on their curriculum problems: problem identification, problem analysis, formulating hypotheses, experimentation and action, and evaluation of results.

But "product" evaluation is another matter in Christian education and must be approached very carefully and delicately. This kind of evaluation may be done by describing resultant behavior (the situation, the results, the product, the outcomes), then asking, "What evidence is there of awareness of God's self-disclosure . . . (referring to the objective and its categories)?" and finally asking, "What does the evidence suggest by way of stages of development, needs, individual difference?" In this last, behavioral indicators by positive and negative clusters might be helpful. Robert J. Havighurst reminds us forcefully, "Religion does bear fruit in a person's life—that fruit can be seen, described, evaluated."

But these behavioral indicators must not be used as curriculum objectives, since this would plunge us into moralism.

Another danger to be avoided is the practice of "evaluating those aspects of Christian education which may be evaluated scientifically and not evaluating those which cannot be evaluated scientifically, important though they be." Such a practice would almost inevitably result in overemphasis on the less important aspects of Christian education, thus producing a distorted picture and practice in the field. We must evaluate rigorously and in detail the things that are our business and evaluate very gingerly (if at all) the things that are not our business.

Individual religious development lends itself to analysis in the form of the case study, in which pertinent materials from tests, anecdotal records, written and oral reports, projective techniques, and interviews with parents and teachers are all used to shed light on the direction of personal development. Such case studies may be done by teachers, counselors, parents, and students, working individually or co-operatively.

Certain aspects of curriculum may best be evaluated by persons not involved in them, especially if detached and objective judgment is necessary. On the other hand, most curriculum situations will best be evaluated co-operatively by the persons most deeply and personally concerned, since the results of their evaluation are most likely to be taken seriously and acted upon.

RESPONSIBILITY FOR CURRICULUM BUILDING

The responsibility for curriculum building, in the deepest sense, is shared by the local parish, the home, the community and its agencies, the denomination, and interdenominational bodies.

The local parish. The local parish provides the locale and the nerve center of the curriculum of Christian education. Here is the teaching-learning process in operation in the Christian community, with all the opportunities for involvement in the life and work of the church. Here is the concern for encounter with integrity with the secular community, and for a parish life that is one of worship, witness, and work. A vital concern for mission and ministry is the heart of the matter. The local parish sets the objective, provides the intellectual rootage, shares a fellowship of believers, stimulates a prophetic outlook, and fosters the ecumenical outlook for the curriculum.

In the light of a parish's commitment to yield itself in such ways to the leading of its Lord, the curriculum of Christian education is planned. Immediately the use of the basic curriculum guide becomes obvious, along with the suggestions and plans found in the area guides and resource units. Out of these an alert parish may shape its teaching program, with the co-operation of its committee or board of Christian education, the staff, the lay leaders, and the participants. One by one, meaningful teaching-learning units are developed or adopted, and settings are devised or adapted to their use.

Herrick and Tyler, speaking of the school situation, comment, "The power and capacity of a school staff to improve its own program grows . . . when (its) working hypotheses are part of the thought and action pattern of each teacher" (p. 124). The same may be said of the church. A parish will be able to build and improve a meaningful and effective program to the extent that all who are a part of it understand and share their concepts of the context, scope, purpose, and process of Christian education.

The home. The home's contribution to the curriculum of Christian education will, by the very nature of its life, be more informal. The home provides the emotional tone for Christian nurture, the basic value system that the learner will be most likely to internalize, the most important laboratory for Christian living, and the family-unit fellowship.

There is no reason why, beginning in a few cases where there is genuine interest, the home cannot share in the planning of basic curriculum experiences with the parish leaders. If this is done slowly and carefully, each home will be able to see its place in the curriculum and will participate through the provision of experiences, resources, and co-operation that otherwise would not have occurred to it.

The community. Community agencies, notably the schools, while not having any direct connection with the curriculum of Christian education in a formal sense, have an important contribution to make. The school provides the basic patterns of education and the fundamental learnings upon which all other aspects of education depend. The school also provides for growing sensitivity and devotion to moral and spiritual values by being, in many of its aspects, a laboratory for the development of character. In addition, the school can teach about certain aspects of religion as a part of the cultural background of the pupil (the religions of the world and the community, great religious leaders, and the Bible as world literature) and can deal with the religious implications in such studies as the social sciences, English, natural sciences, music, and art.

Perhaps even more important, the schools deal with basic themes that help to illuminate the whole field of relationships which Christian education assists the learner to see in the light of the gospel. Such themes, Robert J. Havighurst has pointed out, include the interdependence of the world, the control of nature, the population explosion, the knowledge explosion, and the meaning of the life span and the appropriate use of time throughout the life career.

Other community agencies deal with leisure time, recreation, and character. The focus of our objective is not always the same, yet, these agencies are of marked help in providing for rich and varied experience of the field of relationships, helping the learner to establish broader horizons. Any potential conflict between the church and such agencies may be mitigated by looking at the task "whole" and by continuing mutual search for clarification of our goals.

Denominational and interdenominational agencies. Upon denominational and interdenominational agencies falls direct responsibility for basic curriculum development and supervision.

The basic interdenominational task has long been defined as doing together those things which urgently need to be done but cannot be done unless they are done together, those things which can be done more effectively and economically if they are done together, and certain assigned tasks in such fields as curriculum. This means curriculum outlining, the production of missionary education materials, the production of audiovisual materials, vacation and weekday curriculums, and work with children and youth who are handicapped, gifted, or troubled. On a world scale, it means the development of curriculums like that of the denominations affiliated with the National Christian Council of Japan, the African curriculum, and the curriculum for Spanish-speaking Latin America. City and regional councils of churches have provided for training and fellowship of leaders. Independent groups such as the

Character Research Project at Union College, Schenectady, New York, have been co-operative and helpful to all.

The basic denominational task has been that of producing curriculum materials for all purposes and seeing that they were properly serviced in the local churches. A great deal of pioneering and experimentation in curriculum of various kinds (like curriculum for camps and conferences) has been done by the denominations.

In the light of the suggestions in this book, some additional denominational and interdenominational curriculum duties might be appropriate:

The curriculum guide might be produced interdenominationally, with denominational supplements.

Area guides (perhaps on the eight themes suggested) and resource units (on the age levels and also on an ungraded basis) might be produced interdenominationally, with supplementary units as needed by the denominations.

Denominations or groups of denominations might produce teaching-learning units for local parishes, based upon the resource units.

Parish and teachers' manuals might be produced interdenominationally, with denominational supplements, showing how to make use of the basic curriculum in the parish and in the group.

Denominations might remodel their supervisory services to the local parish so that local churches would be provided with: (1) guidance on the direct use of the curriculum guide, and flexible teaching-learning units, in the construction of their curriculums; (2) adequate servicing of preplanned teaching-learning units.

Local co-operative supervisory plans might be established where feasible.

The conviction is growing that the persons who work at the level of curriculum theory and design and those who work at the level of practice need to work together. There are actually many levels on which curriculum operates: pupils, teachers, groups, leaders, superintendents, directors, pastors, local council people, denominational editors and program people, denominational supervisors, members of boards, and interdenominational staff. As Herrick and Tyler say for education in general: "There must be, on the various levels of curriculum work, people who are consciously trying to see the ideas which are important in clarifying and relating the curriculum activities in their sphere of interest. . . . If a horizontal orientation were established (and at present even this is certainly not a popular current practice), it would then be possible to travel up and down the mountainside to communicate with those who are engaged in different phases of curriculum work and thereby make the essence of their experience and thought available to those who are trying to encompass the whole problem of curriculum theory." (P. 120.)

The individual. The individual himself has the ultimate responsibility for curriculum-building. The curriculum is his, or all the rest of the building is in vain. The curriculum is made or broken on the goals that the individual sets for himself and works toward in company with others or alone. As he asks, "Who am I, really?" the curriculum may help him to answer: "I am a person, created in the image of God but separated from him by sin and in need of reconciliation. I am a member of the human race, with whom God has covenanted, and to whom he has revealed himself. I know who I am because Christ has shown me to myself. I am a man in Christ, an heir of eternal life, a member of Christ's church, and on his mission." The curriculum may help, but the responsibility is his, as God gives him grace to accept that responsibility.

BIBLIOGRAPHY

Allport, Gordon, *Personality: A Psychological Interpretation.* Henry Holt & Co., Inc., 1937.

——— *The Individual and His Religion.* The Macmillan Company, 1950.

——— *Becoming.* Yale University Press, 1955.

Anderson, Vernon E., *Principles and Procedures of Curriculum Improvement.* The Ronald Press Company, 1956.

Arnim, Dorothy, and Sweet, Herman J., *Together We Grow.* Board of Christian Education, Presbyterian Church U.S.A., 1958.

Bathurst, Effie G., *Where Children Live Affects Curriculum.* U.S. Office of Education, 1950.

Betts, George Herbert, *The Curriculum of Religious Education.* Abingdon Press, 1924.

——— *Teaching Religion Today.* Abingdon Press, 1934.

Bloom, Benjamin S. (ed.), *Taxonomy of Educational Objectives: The Classification of Educational Goals (Handbook 1: Cognitive Domain).* Longmans, Green & Co., Inc., 1956.

Bobbitt, Franklin, *How to Make a Curriculum.* Houghton, Mifflin Company, 1924.

Bower, William Clayton, *Character Through Creative Experience.* University of Chicago Press, 1930.

——— *The Curriculum of Religious Education.* Charles Scribner's Sons, 1925.

Bower, William Clayton, and Hayward, Percy R., *Protestantism Faces Its Educational Task Together.* C. C. Nelson Publishing Co., 1949.

Bowman, Clarice M., *Ways Youth Learn*. Harper & Brothers, 1952.

Brubacher, John S., *A History of the Problems of Education*. McGraw-Hill Book Co., Inc., 1947.

Carrier, Blanche, *Free to Grow*. Harper & Brothers, 1951.

Cartwright, Dorwin, and Zander, Alvin, (eds.), *Group Dynamics, Research and Theory*. Row, Peterson & Company, 1953.

Charters, W. W., *The Teaching of Ideals*. The Macmillan Company, 1927.

——— *Curriculum Construction*. The Macmillan Company, 1929.

Chave, Ernest J., *A Functional Approach to Religious Education*. University of Chicago Press, 1947.

Clark, Walter H., *The Psychology of Religion*. The Macmillan Company, 1958.

Coe, George Albert, *A Social Theory of Religious Education*. Charles Scribner's Sons, 1917.

——— *What Is Christian Education?* Charles Scribner's Sons, 1929.

Corson, Fred P., *The Christian Imprint*. Abingdon Press, 1955.

Cully, Iris V., *The Dynamics of Christian Education*. The Westminster Press, 1958.

——— *Children in the Church*. The Westminster Press, 1960.

——— "Is Ecumenical Curriculum Possible?" *Religion in Life*, Summer, 1960. Abingdon Press.

Dewey, John, *Democracy and Education*. The Macmillan Company, 1916.

——— *The Sources of a Science of Education*. Liveright Publishing Corporation, 1929.

Douglass, Truman B., "The Job the Protestants Shirk," *Harpers Magazine*, November, 1958.

Duba, Arlo D., *The Nature and Role of Objectives in Christian Education*. Princeton Theological Seminary, 1955. (Unpublished thesis.)

Elliott, Harrison S., *Can Religious Education Be Christian?* The Macmillan Company, 1940.

Erikson, Erik H., *Childhood and Society*. W. W. Norton & Company, Inc., 1950.

Fallaw, Wesner, *Toward Spiritual Security*. The Westminster Press, 1952.

Forsyth, Nathaniel F., *The Minister and Christian Nurture*. Abingdon Press, 1957.

Frank, Lawrence K., and Frank, Mary, *Your Adolescent at Home and School*. The Viking Press, Inc., 1956.

Frazier, Alexander (ed.), *Learning More About Learning*. Association for Supervision and Curriculum Development, National Education Association, 1959.

French, Will, *Behavioral Goals of General Education in High School*. Russell Sage Foundation, 1957.

Friedman, Maurice, "Martin Buber's 'Theology' and Religious Education," *Religious Education*, January–February, 1959. Published by the Religious Education Association, New York City.

Grimes, Howard, *The Church Redemptive*. Abingdon Press, 1958.

Hall, Calvin S., and Lindzey, Gardner, *Theories of Personality*. John Wiley & Sons, Inc., 1957.

Harris, Chester W. (ed.), *Encyclopedia of Educational Research*, third edition. The Macmillan Company, 1960. Nolan C. Kearney and Walter W. Cook on "Curriculum"; J. Donald Butler on "Religious Education."

Havighurst, Robert J., *Human Development and Education*. Longmans, Green & Co., Inc., 1953.

Heim, Ralph D., *Leading a Sunday Church School*. Muhlenberg Press, 1950.

Herrick, Virgil E., and Tyler, Ralph W., (eds.), *Toward Improved Curriculum Theory*. University of Chicago Press. Copyright 1950 by the University of Chicago.

Hilgard, Ernest R., *Theories of Learning*. Appleton-Century-Crofts, Inc., 1956.

Howe, Reuel L., *Man's Need and God's Action*. The Seabury Press, Inc., 1953.

Hurlock, Elizabeth B., *Developmental Psychology*. McGraw-Hill Book Co., Inc., 1953.

Jaarsma, Cornelius, *Fundamentals in Christian Education Theory and Practice*. Wm. B. Eerdmans Publishing Company, 1953.

Jersild, Arthur T., *Child Development and the Curriculum*. Teachers College Bureau of Publications, 1946.

Kahler, Erich, *The Tower and the Abyss*. George Braziller, Inc., 1957.

Kean, Charles D., *The Christian Gospel and the Parish Church*. The Seabury Press, Inc., 1953.

Kearney, Nolan C., *Elementary School Objectives*. Russell Sage Foundation, 1953.

Kidd, J. R., *How Adults Learn*. Association Press, 1959.

Kilpatrick, William Heard, *Foundations of Method*. The Macmillan Company, 1926.

Kraemer, Hendrick, *The Communication of the Christian Faith*. The Westminster Press, 1956.

————— *A Theology of the Laity*. The Westminster Press, 1958.

Krug, Edward A., *Curriculum Planning* (revised). Harper & Brothers, 1957.

Kuhlen, Raymond G., *The Psychology of Adolescent Development*. Harper & Brothers, 1952.

Lane, Howard, and Beauchamp, Mary, *Human Relations in Teaching*. Prentice-Hall, Inc., 1958.

Lankard, Frank Glenn, *A History of the American Sunday School Curriculum*. Abingdon Press, 1927.

Ligon, Ernest M., *Dimensions of Character*. The Macmillan Company, 1956.

Little, Lawrence C. (ed.), *The Future Course of Christian Adult Education*. University of Pittsburgh, 1959.

McFarland, John T., and Winchester, Benjamin S., (eds.), *The Encyclopedia of Sunday Schools and Religious Education*. Thomas Nelson & Sons, 1915.

Madden, Ward, *Religious Values in Education*. Harper & Brothers, 1951.

Marty, Martin, *The New Shape of American Religion*. Harper & Brothers, 1959.

Maves, Paul V., *Understanding Ourselves as Adults*. Abingdon Press, 1959.

Miller, Allen O., *Invitation to Theology*. Christian Education Press, 1958.

Miller, Park Hays, "Church School Lessons Have a History, Too!" *Growing*, Oct.–Dec., 1948.

Miller, Randolph Crump, *Biblical Theology and Christian Education*. Charles Scribner's Sons, 1956.

————— *The Clue to Christian Education*. Charles Scribner's Sons, 1950.

————— *Education for Christian Living*. Prentice-Hall, Inc., 1956.

Murphy, Gardner, *Personality: A Biosocial Approach to Origins and Structure.* Harper & Brothers, 1947.

———— "Social Motivation," in Lindzey, Gardner (ed.), *Handbook of Social Psychology,* Vol. II. Addison-Wesley Publishing Company, Inc., 1954.

———— *Human Potentialities.* Basic Books, Inc., Publishers, 1958.

Powell, Wilfred Evans, *Education for Life with God.* Abingdon Press, 1934.

Prescott, Daniel A., *The Child in the Educative Process.* Copyright 1957. McGraw-Hill Book Co., Inc. Used by permission.

Pressey, Sidney L., and Kuhlen, Raymond G., *Psychological Development Through the Life Span.* Harper & Brothers, 1957.

Redfield, Robert, *The Educational Experience.* Fund for Adult Education, 1955.

Riesman, David, Glazer, Nathan, and Denny, Reuel, *The Lonely Crowd.* Doubleday Anchor Books, 1954.

Sherrill, Lewis Joseph, *Lift Up Your Eyes.* John Knox Press, 1949.

———— *The Struggle of the Soul.* The Macmillan Company, 1951.

———— *The Gift of Power.* The Macmillan Company, 1955.

Smart, James D., *The Teaching Ministry of the Church.* The Westminster Press, 1954.

———— *The Rebirth of Ministry.* The Westminster Press, 1960.

Strang, Ruth, *The Adolescent Views Himself.* McGraw-Hill Book Co., Inc., 1957.

Stratemeyer, Florence B., and others, *Developing a Curriculum for Modern Living,* second edition revised and enlarged. Teachers College Bureau of Publications, Columbia University, 1957.

Strickland, Ruth G., *How to Build a Unit of Work.* U.S. Office of Education, 1946.

Taba, Hilda, and Noel, Elizabeth, *Action Research: A Case Study.* Association for Supervision and Curriculum Development of the National Education Association, 1957.

Taylor, Marvin (ed.), *Religious Education: A Comprehensive Survey.* Abingdon Press, 1960.

Trow, William Clark, *The Learning Process.* Association for Supervision and Curriculum Development of the National Education Association, 1954.

Vernon, Walter N., "Christian Education in a Stew," *The Christian Century,* October 22, 1958.

Vieth, Paul H., *Objectives in Religious Education*. Harper & Brothers, 1930.

———— *The Church and Christian Education*. The Bethany Press. Copyright 1947. Used by permission.

———— *The Church School*. Christian Education Press, 1957.

Wach, Joachim, *Sociology of Religion*. University of Chicago Press, 1944.

Wick, Julian D., *The Elements in the Design for the Curriculum of Christian Education*. Princeton Theological Seminary, 1959. (Unpublished thesis.)

Wyckoff, D. Campbell, *The Task of Christian Education*. The Westminster Press, 1955.

———— *In One Spirit*. Friendship Press, 1958.

———— *The Gospel and Christian Education*. The Westminster Press, 1959.

———— "Insight—the Key to Help the Adult Worker with Youth Understand His Role in 'Curriculum-Program,'" *Bethany Guide*, April, 1959; "Planning Program-Curriculum," *Bethany Guide*, May, 1959.

Yeaxlee, Basil A., *Religion and the Growing Mind*. The Seabury Press, Inc., 1952.

Zubek, John P., and Solberg, P. A., *Human Development*. McGraw-Hill Book Co., Inc., 1954.

The Aims of Religious Education, Proceedings of the Third Annual Convention of the Religious Education Association. Religious Education Association, 1905.

Learning and the Teacher. Association for Supervision and Curriculum Development of the National Education Association, 1959.

A Look at Continuity in the School Program, 1958 yearbook. Washington, D.C.: Association for Supervision and Curriculum Development, a department of the National Education Association, 1958.

One Hundred Years of Curriculum Improvement, 1857–1957. Association for Supervision and Curriculum Development of the National Education Association, 1957.

Research for Curriculum Improvement. Association for Supervision and Curriculum Development of the National Education Association, 1957.

The Unit in Curriculum Development and Research. Bureau of Curriculum Research, Board of Education of the City of New York, 1956.

Publications of the National Council of the Churches of Christ in the U.S.A., and its predecessor, the International Council of Religious Education:
The Development of a Curriculum of Religious Education, 1928 (revised, 1930).
The International Curriculum Guide, 1932.
    Book I: *Principles and Objectives of Christian Education.*
    Book II: *Christian Education of Children.*
    Book III: *Christian Education of Youth.*
    Book VI: *The Organization and Administration of Christian Education in the Local Church.*
Christian Education Today, 1940.
The Study of Christian Education, 1946–1947.
The Curriculum Guide for the Local Church, 1945 (revised, 1950).
Junior High Objectives, 1953.
A Guide for Curriculum in Christian Education, 1955.
The Objectives of Christian Education, 1958.
The Objective of Christian Education for Senior High Young People, 1958.
Evaluation and Christian Education, 1960.

Selected denominational documents in curriculum theory and design:
LUTHERAN (four bodies), Philadelphia, Pennsylvania:
The Objectives of Christian Education, 1957.
The Age-Level Objectives of Christian Education, 1958.
The Functional Objectives for Christian Education. Copyright 1959 by W. Kent Gilbert. Used by permission.

METHODIST, Nashville, Tennessee:
A Manual on Goals and Materials for Christian Teaching, 1959 (revised).
Foundations of Christian Teaching in Methodist Churches, 1960. Used by permission.

PRESBYTERIAN U.S., Richmond, Virginia:
Christian Education Within the Covenant Community—the Church,
1958.

PROTESTANT EPISCOPAL, Greenwich, Connecticut:
The Church's Teaching Series (6 vols.)

UNITED CHURCH OF CANADA, Toronto, Ontario, Canada:
Presuppositions.
"Curriculum: Its Organizing Principle, Plan, and Unit Descriptions,"
a working paper, July 3, 1959.

UNITED CHURCH OF CHRIST, Boston, Massachusetts, and Philadelphia,
Pennsylvania:
*A Statement of Educational Principles as Seen in the Light of
Christian Theology and Beliefs,* 1957.

UNITED PRESBYTERIAN, Philadelphia, Pennsylvania:
*Basic Principles: An Official Statement on the Christian Faith and
Life Curriculum,* 1947.
Christian Faith and Life at a Glance (Revised), 1958.

Index

INDEX

Action research, 198–199

Administration, 26–27, 78–79, 181–182, 197–200

Adolescence, 109

Adulthood, 109

Allport, Gordon, 96, 97

American Baptist Convention, 10, 76

American Lutheran Church, The, 10

American Sunday School Union, 32

Anderson, Vernon E., 43

Anticipated behavioral outcomes, 62, 68–70, 79, 185, 197

Area guide, 186, 187, 189–192, 194, 203

Arnim, Dorothy, 96

Association for Supervision and Curriculum Development, 43–44, 165–167

Barth, Karl, 51

Bathurst, Effie G., 178–179

Beauchamp, Mary, 109

Betts, George Herbert, 33–34, 35

Bible, 54, 95, 114, 117, 129, 153–154, 172, 173, 174

Bonhoeffer, Dietrich, 51

Bower, William Clayton, 34–35

Bowman, Clarice M., 97

Broad grading, 168

Buber, Martin, 51, 93–94, 147–148

Carrier, Blanche, 96

Cartwright, Dorwin, 109

Character Research Project, 202–203

Childhood, 108

Christian, definition of, 22

Christian education, 20–25, 155–157; requirements for, 25–26

Christian Faith and Life: A Program for Church and Home. See The United Presbyterian Church in the U.S.A.

Church, 18–20, 26, 31–32, 59–60, 83, 89, 114–121, 131–137, 138–146, 146–155, 163–164, 172–177, 181–182, 185, 200–204; ministries of, 20–21

Church of the Brethren, 10

215